MORE
GARDEN
WOODWORK
in a
WEEKEND

MORE
GARDEN
WOODWORK
in a
WEEKEND

RICHARD BLIZZARD

David and Charles

NOTE FROM THE AUTHOR

To ensure that everyone can have a go at them, the projects in *More Garden Woodwork in a Weekend* are graded for varying levels of skill. They encompass designs suitable for beginners, a selection of intermediate projects and finally more complex challenges for the advanced woodworker. It is always advisable to begin with the simpler projects if you are new to woodworking, and tackle the more complex ones as your confidence grows. You will learn new skills and techniques as you work your way through each project, and gain experience of how to get the most out of your tools and equipment.

Throughout the book, there is a variety of designs suitable for gardens both large and small, and I am sure you will find several to enhance your own outdoor space. I have thoroughly enjoyed working on the projects in this book, and whether you choose one with a practical function, or one that is purely for pleasure, I hope that you enjoy making and using them as much as I have.

RICHARD BLIZZARD

A DAVID & CHARLES BOOK
Copyright © David & Charles Limited 2002, 2008

David & Charles is an F+W Publications Inc. company
4700 East Galbraith Road
Cincinnati, OH 45236

First published in 2002
First UK paperback edition 2008

Text copyright © Richard Blizzard 2002, 2008

Richard Blizzard has asserted his right to be identified as author of this work in accordance with the Copyright, Designs and Patents Act, 1988.

A catalogue record for this book is available from the British Library.

ISBN-13: 978-0-7153-1193-6 hardback
ISBN-10: 0-7153-1193-X hardback

ISBN-13: 978-0-7153-2880-4 paperback
ISBN-10: 0-7153-2880-8 paperback

Printed in China by R R Donnelley
for David & Charles
Brunel House, Newton Abbot, Devon

Commissioning Editor: Fiona Eaton
Desk Editor: Jennifer Proverbs
Art Editor: Diana Dummet
Photography: Perception Photography

The author has made every effort to ensure that all of the instructions in this book are accurate and safe, and therefore cannot accept liability for any resulting injury, damage or loss to persons or property, however it may arise.

Visit our website at www.davidandcharles.co.uk

David & Charles books are available from all good bookshops; alternatively you can contact our Orderline on 0870 9908222 or write to us at FREEPOST EX2 110, D&C Direct, Newton Abbot, TQ12 4ZZ (no stamp required UK only); US customers call 800-289-0963 and Canadian customers call 800-840-5220.

CONTENTS

INTRODUCTION TO TOOLS AND MATERIALS

Technology has transformed the traditional ways of woodworking and made it possible for home owners to create their own furniture from wood. Battery powered screwdrivers, hand-saws with razor-sharp teeth that don't need re-sharpening, and chisels with 'comfy-fit' handles are just some of the technological innovations to benefit woodworkers. In addition, scientists have invented water-resistant glues, and wood stains now not only give a wonderful colour and finish, but will protect your garden projects for years to come.

The tools and materials I have recommended here are the same ones I use myself, and trust to do an outstanding job – but they are only a guide. There are many factors to consider when purchasing tools. Take your time – there is no need to buy everything at once, although a full set is always something to aim for. Seek advice and information on what is available and take your time choosing. My own advice would be to buy the best tools and materials you can afford. Good quality purchases will pay for themselves in the long run and help you to create woodwork projects of which you can be proud.

Now I will guide you through the range of hand and power tools, glues, timber and finishing products that I think are useful for the projects, and for successful woodworking in general.

HAND TOOLS

There is absolutely no compromise for quality tools and I recommend Stanley tools, as they will not only last your lifetime, but they are definitely second-generation tools: leave them to your children in your Will.

If you think hand tools have changed little in the past ten years, you are in for a surprise. Tool makers are innovative and imaginative, and are capable of responding rapidly to the different materials that come on the market that require cutting, drilling or planing. I can hardly think of a single hand tool in the Stanley range that has not been improved (except maybe the bradawl). So here is what Stanley has to offer you.

Stanley hand tools

With this selection of Stanley hand tools, you will have all you need to complete the projects in the book.

Panel Saw

Jetcut saws were introduced some eight to ten years ago. The teeth of these saws have three sharp faces, do not blunt easily, and cut on both pull and push strokes. There are fine-tooth saws, ideal for the projects in this book, and the not so fine, when you want to convert a plank rapidly. The very latest is the 'all-black' Teflon-coated saw, which reduces friction when you saw – so more speed and less arm ache.

The blade and handle are arranged so that you can use them as a 45-degrees and 90-degrees set square – mind the teeth, as they are like those of a piranha fish. The handles are made from a semi-hard compound that makes them far less tiring to use than many of the 'plastic' handles on the market. Razor-sharp teeth, set-square handle, superb, fine-cut finish and a non-stick blade – it is a veritable space-age saw!

Tenon Saw

For all those small accurate cuts, a tenon saw is a must. They come from the same stable as the Jetcut saws, so they are sharp, and remain so for the life of the saw. No Teflon coating yet, but I am sure that is just around the corner.

Carpenter's Squares

Here the choice varies from the least expensive, plastic-handled carpenter's try square, to the really nicely set up 'combination' square. For some of the garden projects I am loath to take my really good square out of the workshop, so I rely on the least expensive one. However, you will find the combination square very, very useful. The blade acts as a rule, and the foot of the square acts as a spirit level.

A two-in-one tool like this is great. With all big outdoor jobs – the decking described in this book is a good example – it is helpful to have a really big square. Like many other people, I have made triangles from old battens to form a 90-degree square. Now Stanley has produced a big folding square. It is quick to use when you want to check that the job is still at 90-degrees, making it a useful tool for the garden, and when you have finished, it simply folds away.

Hammers

Hammers must surely be the most abused tool in any household, being used for everything from cracking concrete to levering off a tyre. Many decades ago, Stanley perfected the method of keeping a hammer's head on, but not until very

recently did they produce an 'antivibe' hammer. Striking nails into timber creates shock waves from the head of the hammer along the shaft, through the hand and wrist, and on up into the elbow. Some of us know about the pain induced by tennis elbow, and so are grateful that the redesigned antivibe hammer shaft goes a long way to prevent more elbow damage. It reduces vibration because the end of the hammer handle is split like a tuning fork – when the shock wave comes along the hammer shaft, it is dissipated in the fork end – very innovative. The latest hammers have the antivibe handle, and are also far more carefully shaped than ever before.

Clamps

Remember the old cast-iron 'G' clamps that took forever to wind up? Well, the latest design has a quick-release mechanism. The screw-handle section slides along the clamp bar's serrated edge. When you clamp an object, the sliding bar automatically locks on the serrations, and you then tighten up the screw handle to lock the object in the clamp's jaws. These clamps come in a variety of sizes and have nylon covers over their jaws, preventing marking the timber.

Staple Guns

Unlike the humble home stapler, these staple guns can whack in some huge staples. Not only do they fire staples, but they can also be loaded with brad nails, and in this format will fix light trellis battens together.

Surform Tools

This is one of those tools that often tends to get overlooked, so if you have not tried one, do – it is a valuable piece of kit. These are an excellent substitute for sandpaper and other tools used for removing excess material from a surface. I generally go for the moulded body plane, which gives good results. The sole is made up of hundreds of small curved teeth that cut away unwanted material at speed. There is a variety of different shaped surform tools, and even a round file.

Smoothing Planes

The smoothing plane is a piece of Stanley tradition, yet even this most beautiful of woodworking tools has seen a steady development. Properly sharpened, with the cap iron correctly set, it will give you the most wonderful cut; in fact the shavings come off the timber as easily as when you peel an apple with a penknife. There is real music to be heard as the smoothing plane swishes to and fro, the tightly curled shavings spilling out of its mouth. In fact, anyone who knows planes can tell you with their eyes closed if the one being used is sharp or blunt. A sharp plane cuts timber with a clean whistling sound – try it!

Drills

When I was a boy, one of my first tools was a Stanley hand drill with twin pinions – it was my pride and joy, and I still have it. There is something rather special about boring and countersinking holes, and a hand drill gives you the opportunity to be in absolute control. I have to admit that I bore few holes with my old drill, but I do keep a countersink in the chuck for jobs that require a very delicate touch.

Chiselers

You cannot get started on these 'weekend' projects without a good set of chisels. The Dynagrip Pro chisels are beautifully crafted, and I suggest a boxed set of three is probably the least expensive way of buying them. This will give you a range of sizes – ½in, ¾in, 1in – which is adequate. Buying a boxed set also means

Rolling tool store
Stanley's superb compact rolling tool store – a place for everything.

that you get a very strong moulded case to keep them in, which prevents the cutting edges getting blunted.

The handles are beautifully made from a rubber compound that is very comfortable to hold. Now, chisels should never be struck with a hammer, always a mallet, but there are those who will misuse their tools, and Stanley, who is in the fight to keep its chisels looking good, has fitted protective metal caps on the handle tops.

There is a very good reason why it is best to use a wooden mallet for chisel work, and it has to do with the safety of your hands. A mallet has a large head, with its striking face cut at an angle. This large head makes it very difficult for you to miss the chisel handle and clang your knuckles instead. A hammer head is small, and when you miss the top of the chisel, as you inevitably will, your hand will suffer some nasty bruising. Be safe, and be kind to yourself and your chisels – go and get a mallet.

CHISEL SHARPENER AND OILSTONE

To keep your chisels sharp, a honing guide and oilstone are absolutely essential. The honing guide is effectively a clamp with wheels that holds the chisel at the correct angle for sharpening. Spray a light oil, such as WD40, on the oilstone and push the clamped chisel to and fro on the oilstone. One of the tell-tale signs that the stone and oil are forming a cutting edge is the colour of the oil – it changes to black. Plastic chisel caps are available to prevent your chisel edges getting accidentally damaged when stored.

Rolling Tool Store

I am sure that you will be thinking about where on earth all these tools will be kept. Well here's the answer. Stanley has just invented the most versatile toolbox. This rolling tool store is well thought out and designed, with a place for everything and everything in it's place. Provision is even made for a cable drum and panel saws, and the handle is a great help when you are getting your tool kit on site.

POWER TOOLS

Power tools are an absolute necessity for the majority of jobs you do around the home and garden. Try drilling into concrete without a percussion hammer drill – it would take you hours, and it is quite likely the job would defeat you. A traditional hand plane produces the finest surface, but if you have hundreds of feet of sawn timber to plane up to make garden furniture, then the electric hand-held plane is by far the best and fastest choice.

Hand and power tools compliment each other, and when you begin to use power tools, you will wonder how you ever did without them. If I had to choose just two power tools to begin with, then it would be a battery/drill screwdriver and a jigsaw – these two pieces of equipment can achieve so much for you.

Cordless Drill/Screwdriver – Bosch Model PSR 9.6VE2

If you are fairly new to woodworking, you may not be familiar with these tools. Nearly everybody has heard of battery tools, but many have not tried them, and are under the illusion that the battery resembles something like their old bicycle battery. Nothing could be further from the truth. So what is a cordless drill/screwdriver and what will it do?

BATTERY

The batteries in all these machines are rechargeable, and the drill comes with a battery charger. The charging unit is plugged into the mains, the battery pushed into the charging unit (you cannot put it in the wrong way round) and, once turned on, a green indicator light flashes as it charges and remains constant when it is fully charged. This battery does need care, as it is a very advanced piece of technology, so read the instructions.

Now one of the great advantages of a battery tool is that you can do jobs without the restriction of a cable. The shed needs a board re-screwed, the fence at the bottom of the garden needs attention – both of these can be done without trailing yards of mains cable behind you. Also the sheer torque (turning power) that the machine delivers will amaze you – these 9.6-volt batteries simply do not run out of power.

Bosch battery drill/screwdriver
Two speeds and a range of torque settings will give you all the power you need.

DRILL OR DRIVER?

When is a drill not a drill? When it is operating as a screwdriver. If you want to bore a hole in timber, perspex, concrete, or whatever, you need a variable speed control. Holes drilled in wood generally require a higher speed than those in, say, mild steel, where the speed is best kept fairly low. The drill is fitted with an electronic speed control that will accelerate from zero to maximum just by squeezing the trigger. With this total speed control comes the ability to make the drill work as a screwdriver, too. Screws need to be driven fairly slowly into timber – if you tried to drive a screw in at, say, 2000 revolutions, then you and the screw would have a problem. However, with the screw started in the wood, all that is required is a steady hand pressure on the handle of the drill and slow revolutions, and the screw is on its way. It is probably true to say that the turning power of one of these drills is far above the turning power of the average wrist (unless you are a blacksmith).

Now screws, as we know, come in a vast variety of sizes, and it is obvious that a 3in (70mm) screw will need more energy to drive into the timber than one only 1in (25mm) long. To accommodate this there is a torque or slip clutch control that has several settings to accommodate the different size screws. A knurled ring around the front of the tool controls the torque settings. The different settings are graduated and clearly shown. It also shows you the position to turn to, to lock off the clutch and set the drill/screwdriver into the drill mode only.

9

GEARBOX

To make the most of the machine's power, a two-speed mechanical gearbox is fitted. This will enable you to get the maximum torque at low speeds.

BRAKES

We have become used to some very sophisticated braking systems in our cars, and this drill has a brake to prevent 'run on' when you stop squeezing the trigger. In other words, it stops instantly. Its purpose? Well, you can easily snap the head off a screw once it is fully driven home, if you cannot stop screwing immediately.

CHUCKS

In the not-so-distant past, all drills had keys to tighten their chucks, but no longer. This single-sleeve, key-less chuck is simplicity to use, and you can change from a drill to a screwdriver in seconds.

HANDLE

You may get blisters, but not from this machine handle, which is made from a material that gives ever so slightly when you grip it firmly.

LOST IT/FOUND IT

If you are one of those people who put things down and then cannot find them, there is a magnet for you to stick the drill bits or whatever on to the top of the drill.

This one machine alone will save you hours of work, and will enable you to tackle jobs that you would not have had the confidence to try before.

Jigsaw – Bosch Model PST 550AE

I am sure they have their origins in cutting wooden jigsaw puzzles, but I suspect that 90 percent of all jigsaws sold nowadays never get near a jigsaw puzzle. The jigsaw has been developed so much that it has almost become the universal cutting tool. Builders, plumbers, shop fitters, boat builders, electricians – all carry one in the back of their trucks. So what can it do for you in speeding up the making of your garden furniture?

CHUNKY CUT

The Bosch 550 is the smallest jigsaw in the range, but it is capable of cutting through timber to a depth of $2^{1}/_{2}$in (65mm) – in other words, it will do all the cutting jobs for the projects in this book.

It is not just wood that a jigsaw will cut efficiently. Bosch makes a huge range of blades for every material: choose the correct blade, and the little machine will tackle mild steel, plastic pipe, perspex and all the man-made plyboards, chipboard and so on. One of the most interesting blades to try is the 'Progressor' blade. This cuts timber very efficiently and leaves virtually no visible saw marks. Normally after sawing, the timber has to be sanded or otherwise smoothed, to remove the jagged saw-cut marks, but the 'Progressor' blade does away with this necessity.

CURVY LINES

Jigsaws have been associated with cutting shapes, scrolls, circles and so forth, and yes, they are particularly suited to this type of work. However, they can also follow a straight line, and I frequently use mine for slicing up sheets of plywood, as the tool is lightweight and easily manoeuvred. The sole plate of the machine can be canted at an angle for mitre cuts – there are graduated angles printed in the sole plate for your guidance. The sole plate is also adjustable and can be moved backwards, which is very useful if you need to cut right up to a wall, for example.

Bosch jigsaw
With the correct blade fitted, this jigsaw will cut almost any material.

HUFF AND PUFF

As you cut, lots of small timber particles are removed from the timber/board that you are cutting. These must be brushed away from the blade, as they obscure the pencil line that you are following. This machine has an in-built blower that does the job for you. The fine dust created by jigsaws can be very hazardous, so the machine has an in-built dust extraction facility. Link the jigsaw to a hose and dust extractor unit and you will not only prevent dust getting into circulation in the shed, you will also avoid breathing it in.

THE CLICK

One of the most frustrating widgets on older jigsaws was the blade-securing mechanism. A clamp and two screws, and yes, as you changed the blade you dropped the screws in the shavings beneath the bench. Gone are the fiddly screws and clamps, and on the modern Bosch jigsaws, all you do is offer the blade up, and the spring-loaded mechanism automatically locks it into the plunger arm. Removal of the blade is just as simple.

HANDS ON

Other features of this well-engineered jigsaw include a 450-watt motor, a small roller guide behind the blade to give it support, and a slide-down perspex blade cover, just in case your hand slips off the top of the machine while you are working.

Router – Bosch Model POF 400A

The router is surely one of the most versatile of woodworking machines: in the hands of an experienced woodworker with an imaginative flair, it could be said to be almost universal in the joints it can cut and the timber it can shape. Traditionally, the carpenter used his router to check that the bottoms of housing joints were flat across their entire length. Cutters of different widths were supplied and this two-handed implement was part of the furniture in any workshop until about ten years ago. This 'son' of router is really a hyperactive, do-almost-anything machine. I am told that, due to the noise they make

and their very high cutting speed, most routers languish on the shelf. Don't let yours.

The little 400-watt Bosch machine stacks up well compared to some of the larger and more exotic ones available. I find it a delight to use. It is not a heavyweight, it fits well in the hands, and performs without vibrating. The on/off switch is positioned in the handle, so you can turn off, keeping both hands on the handles – always a good idea, given that the machine you have can cut at 20,000 revolutions a minute. It can also cut to a depth of 2in (48mm), and glides across the timber on its non-stick base as if on ice!

Reducing it to its basic parts, the machine has an electric motor that is mounted vertically and has a shaft leading from it to a chuck at the bottom (the business end). There are two handles to control the router, a fence for rebate work and a micro-adjuster for setting the cutter to the exact depth. There is also the all-important dust-extraction adapter for connecting to a vacuum cleaner, which is a must, unless you want lights on the machine to see where you are going through the chippings and dust.

So what can you use it for? Well, many of the basic woodworking jobs can be done with it, depending on the cutters you buy for specific tasks and your understanding of some of the possibilities.

Bosch 'baby' electric router
Perfect for 'shaping up' timbers, and also an ideal first router.

12

REBATES

Choose the size of cutter, and either with the parallel fence fixed or with a ball bearing to guide the cutter, off you go.

HOUSINGS

If the parallel fence has not got sufficient length to reach the central section of the timber, use a straight-edge batten, and align the batten and router with the housing joint to be cut.

SHAPING AND PROFILING

One of the most satisfying jobs to do with a router is to shape the square edges of timber. There are literally dozens of profiles to choose from. These router bits normally have a ball bearing on their tip and, as you work, this guides the cutter along the edge of the timber, following its contour. The ball bearing allows the tip of the cutter to rotate, without burning the timber – ingenious! I have used this type of cutter in some of the projects in this book; if you look at the garden bench you will see how it is used, and the difference it makes to the overall appearance.

TEMPLATES

A router will cut out almost any shape for you, provided that you have a method of guiding it. For example, if you have a straight rebate cutter, you fit a housing around it and a template for the housing to follow, and the router will cut out internal shapes. Staircase sides are made in this way, and work-top surfaces can be cut and fitted neatly using a template.

CARVING

Those with a gift for sketching or drawing can use routers to carve a picture.

Electric Planer – Bosch Model (with bag) PHO 16–82

When trees are sawn into planks at the sawmill, the circular saws or band mills leave a rough surface. For some garden projects this rough surface is helpful, because the wood preservative sticks far better to the rough-sawn fibres than it does to a

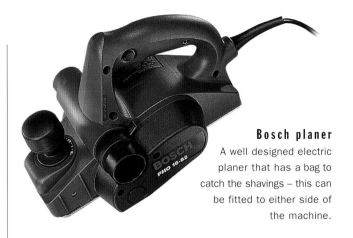

Bosch planer
A well designed electric planer that has a bag to catch the shavings – this can be fitted to either side of the machine.

smooth, planed surface. Sawn timbers are fine, therefore, for arches, trellis work and border edgings; however, when you want to make, say, a garden bench, then you really need to have planed timber. Planed timber is more expensive than the sawn variety because the mills have the extra process to put all the wood through. If time is not a factor for you, then planing up your own timber will certainly save money.

The Stanley bench planes do a superb job and are absolutely indispensable to any workshop, but if you intend to buy and plane up hundreds of feet of timber, it will take time and a great deal of energy, and this is where the electric hand-held planer is ideal. It will save you literally hours of work and the Bosch machines do produce a very good finish.

CLEAN SHAVE

The electric planer works on a different principle to the Stanley bench plane. It has a circular block in which is set a single blade. One-bladed cutter blocks are, I believe, unique to the Bosch machine. You might think that one blade would impede progress, but this is not the case, and the finish is silky smooth.

When the machine is working, the block spins at high revolutions and the blade takes small chippings or shavings from the timber. The cutting depth is controlled by a circular knob at the front of the machine and at full adjustment will remove up to 1.6mm in one pass. The motor is 550 watt and delivers the power very smoothly. Just try removing 1.6mm of shavings from a 6ft (1.2m) length of timber using a hand plane and you will realize just how powerful and efficient the electric plane is.

DUST UP

One of the things you discover immediately is the snowstorm of shavings that the planer shoots out and the machine comes as standard with a dust bag. One of the frustrating things in the past was that the dust bag fitted on one side only, so if you were working against a wall, it got in the way. But with this machine, the bag can be fitted on either side, and a clever 'gate' has been devised to divert the shavings in the right direction, straight into the bag.

GROOVY

In some of projects, it is a good idea to remove the edge of the timber. For example, with garden benches and chairs, the slats you sit on can be uncomfortable, unless you plane away the corners. This plane has a groove milled in its front table. If you set a piece of timber in the vice, the groove locates onto the 90-degree edge, and makes planing it away simplicity.

PARKING UP

If you have ever been in a cabinetmaker's or a carpenter's shop, you will know that to put a hand plane face down (blade down) is a crime: you must always put the plane on its side so the blade and its setting will not be damaged. However, if you do forget, nothing too drastic happens, other than a slapped wrist. But if you forget with an electric planer – *ie* you put it down with the blade spinning – it takes a chunk out of the bench, usually knocks the blade about, and gives you a shock. This planer has a very natty 'shoe' that automatically drops into place, thus preventing damage to you and the machine. It is one of those little bits of design that makes this a really useful tool.

REBATES

It is very useful to have a machine that not only planes the boards, but can take it a stage further, by cutting rebates. The plane can rebate up to a depth of ¼in (8mm) and a maximum width of 3¼in (82mm). The rebate fences and stops come separately; they do not come as standard.

Orbital Sander – Bosch Model PSS 240A

Orbital sanders have contributed enormously to the quality of finish that it is possible to get on timber. As any DIY enthusiast will tell you, they tackle not just bare timber, but are excellent for rubbing down old paintwork and even plaster. My first impressions of these machines was how much work you could get done with a relatively small piece of glasspaper, in comparison to how many sheets you use when rubbing down by hand. The smooth finish is achieved by the sanding pad being moved not just in one direction, but orbitally. This prevents unsightly scratches on the work surface.

The sanding sheets can be changed rapidly with the 'hook and loop' system, which is rather like velcro. A 'lock on' button is provided, so that you do not get thumb ache on those long sanding jobs. There are different sanding sheet sizes. This sander has a $1/3$ sheet system and the motor is matched so the work progresses quickly.

Bosch orbital sander
This orbital sander incorporates a micro-filter system to trap the smallest particles of dust. It is simply the cleanest sander I know.

BIG DUST UP

For me, the revolutionary change in orbital sanders has been in the removal of dust. Look back ten years and these machines were being produced without dust bags. They produce a very fine dust, which not only completely smothers the workshop, but is also freely inhaled. Bosch has come up with something better than the dust bag: it has developed a stunning miniaturized dust-extraction system, called a micro filter. The motor not only drives the sanding pad, but also works a small fan that draws the dust through the holes in the sander base plate and pushes it into the micro filter, which traps and holds it.

14

When the filter is full, it can be opened and the dust removed. This system is a very big advance in preventing quantities of potentially damaging dust particles getting into our lungs and working environment.

Circular Saw – Bosch Model PKS 46

You may feel that a circular saw is a bit daunting to use, but it is one of those machines that fully equips you to convert large quantities of timber to any size you want. It is undoubtedly the fastest and most accurate way to make straight and angled cuts, and really equips the home workshop to tackle any DIY job. It allows you to take advantage of job lots of timber at the merchants; you can also buy large timber stock and then convert it with your circular saw to the sizes that best suit your project. If you are planning a large project that requires ply- or chipboard to be sliced up, then this is the machine for the job.

BIG CUT

The heart of any saw is its blade and this one comes with a 6in (15mm) tungsten carbide blade. Now, tungsten-tipped blades really are necessary when cutting man-made boards. They stay sharp for many hundreds of hours longer than a conventional blade, and the 620-watt motor has all the power you need to propel the blade rapidly through whatever material you need to cut. It slices through melamine kitchen work tops or makes angles on ends, like a cheese cutter.

If you have large boards to cut, then do make sure that you support the board on either side of the cut.

Bosch circular saw
Large quantities of timber can be rapidly cut to size with this machine, which has a versatile adjustable cutting depth.

Failure to do this may mean that the board near the end of the cut pinches the blade of the saw, spoiling your neat cut and endangering you. Before you start any cut, think it through. Are there any obstacles in the way? Can I complete the cut in one pass? What will happen to the cable as I progress the cut? Is it likely to get in the way? And, of course, safety specs are absolutely vital to prevent any eye damage.

MITRE CUT

A movable base plate swivels over to a maximum of 45 degrees, and you will be absolutely amazed at the accuracy of the cut. A guide fence is provided. It locks into the sole plate, and is fully adjustable.

DEPTH CUT

The depth at which the saw cuts can also be quickly adjusted, from a massive 2in (46mm) to zero. This allows the rapid cutting of housing joints across planks, and enables you to get the most productive cut from different thicknesses of planks.

SAFETY FEATURES

A great deal of thought has gone into making this machine safe to use:
- Well-positioned handles for a two-hand hold
- Large sole plate giving the machine maximum stability
- Spring-loaded saw guard keeps the blade guarded on both sides until it begins to cut the timber
- Twin rollers fitted to the spring-loaded guard means that the transition from guarded blade to cutting mode is made without any potentially damaging jerks or snatches
- Substantial riving knife behind the blade prevents the timber closing on the blade after the saw has passed through

DUST EXTRACTION

Provision is made in the guard to take a dust-extractor nozzle or an optional dust bag. I would suggest that you always use one or the other, because these saws can create great clouds of damaging dust particles.

MAINTENANCE

You must keep the blade clean. Do not allow deposits of resin or gum from the timber to build up around the tungsten-tipped teeth – WD40 is a good cleaning agent. At the first sign of the blade blunting off, take it back to your Bosch dealer, who will arrange for it to be re-sharpened. You cannot re-sharpen carbide teeth with a smooth-cut file – they are too hard.

Conclusion

These power tools will enable you to make some wonderful projects. They will inspire you to tackle jobs that you might have thought impossible. After use, discipline yourself to clean them – give them a squirt of WD40 and wipe it off with a cloth. They are tools to be proud of and they will give many years of first-class work. I suspect from the quality of build that they will survive to be passed to a second generation of power tool woodworkers.

STANLEY BOSTITCH PNEUMATIC NAILERS

In industry, compressor-driven tools have been around for a very long time. Although powered by a stream of compressed air, they often look similar to their electrical contemporaries. In America, these tools have been available to the general DIY consumer for a long time, but it is only with the growth of DIY programmes on television, particularly those showing decking being 'nailed down', that they have come to the attention of the general public.

The great institution that has made industrial tools accessible to us all is, of course, the tool-hire shop. These shops will provide you with everything from a scaffold rig to a concrete mixer, and those who work there can give advice on the best tools for different jobs.

Nailer Air-Tool – Model SB-1842BN

The first tool – and often the only one – that many people purchase is a hammer, or brad nailer. Hammering is something we begin to master at

infancy. No other tool feels as natural to use, or conveys its purpose quite like a hammer. My first tool was a small Stanley hammer. Stanley now make a huge variety of tools that work from compressed air.

These 'air tools' are taking over from the traditional hammer, as they can drive nails (brads) faster and indeed more accurately than the traditional hammers. The very latest 'combination' air tool has a magazine that takes five different sizes of staple and nail all in one tool. The really huge jumbo 'stick' nailers are ideal for roofing timbers.

HOW IT WORKS

A piston and cylinder are inside the body of the hammer. When the trigger is depressed, a jet of compressed air drives the piston, which strikes a drive rod with great force, and this is what activates the 'hammering' of the nail or 'brad' into the timber. The piston travels through a complete cycle and returns to the top of the cylinder, ready to strike again when you are ready.

The brad nailer is connected by a flexible air line to a compressor, which supplies the necessary compressed air. A fairly small sized compressor will run even a big nailer. The brads are held in a clip-type magazine, which is spring-loaded, feeding the brads to be fired whenever the trigger on the nailer is depressed.

Stanley Nailer Air-Tool

A small compressor and flexible hose (not shown) provide the nail gun with compressed air.

The most versatile of the Stanley air tools is the SB 2 in 1 Combi Brad Nailer. The magazine in this tool accepts a total of five different sizes of staple and seven different brad (nail) sizes.

ITS ADVANTAGES

Every time you pull the trigger on a brad nailer, you are saving yourself a lot of time and effort: think of all the blows it takes to drive in a nail. In addition, hammering constantly pounds the structure you are making, whereas with an air-tool, it is not shaken at all. This is an important consideration, particularly if you want to do accurate work. If you want to build a decking rapidly, then it is possible to do it in just a day with the nailer.

WHAT ARE BRADS?

Brads are a development on traditional nails. They are rectangular with T-shaped heads and slightly blunted V-shaped tips. Most are coated with a resin glue that increases their grip in the timber. They come in clips that are ready to load into the magazine, not unlike the staples used in a domestic staple gun.

The brad has several advantages over the traditional nail; among these are that it is smaller and so leaves a less noticeable hole, and the fact that as the blunted tip punches a hole, it is far less likely to split the wood. The traditional nail has to be larger as it withstands numerous blows, whereas the brad is driven in by a single blow.

THREE-IN-ONE FOR PRECISION WORK

In fact, the brad nailer combines three tools – drill, countersink and hammer. The tool is lightweight, and once positioned on the timber, makes for a 'sure fix' every time. Until I was working on the projects for this book, I had not fully appreciated just how delicate a job the brad nailer can perform – it is perfect for fixing small mouldings.

The brads can be driven in close to the edge of a moulding without the fear of huge, unsightly splits. The manufacturer provides the tip of the nailer with a 'rubber boot', which helps to prevent the tool marking the faces of the delicate mouldings.

Safety

It is essential to wear protective eye gear. One of the dangers with the air-tool is the exhaust port. When the trigger is depressed and then released, a charge of air exhausts from this port. If you happen to be working in a confined space, the sudden jet of air can blow chippings and dust and so on into your face and eyes. Also, because brads are made from soft steel, there is a tendency for them to bend if they encounter something very hard in the timber, such as a knot.

Sometimes the brad will shoot out of the wood, although this is a very rare occurrence. However, as a precaution, to help prevent this happening, the tip or nose of the nailer should be held absolutely perpendicular to the outside edge of the wood. Thus any side-to-side deflection of the brad is thereby safely contained in the wood. The brad will follow the angle that the tool is tilted at, so always try to hold the nailer level with the surface of the timber.

It is a good idea not only to protect your eyes, but also your ears, as the big brad nailers can exceed 80 decibels (DB).

TIMBER

The basic raw material for this book is timber, and I have tried to design items from stock-size timbers. However, there is a whole new vocabulary to be learned when talking about timber: for example, P.S.E. (planed square edge), and T&G board (tongue-and-groove board).

There are many different grades of timber, joinery quality being the most expensive. If not your builder's merchant, then certainly one of the big DIY stores will keep edge-laminated pine, which forms the basis of items such as the Indoor Pebble Pool (page 38). Edge-laminated pine boards are available in a huge variety of sizes. They are made up from small strips of pine glued together to form large boards. The strips of pine glued together in this way are quite flat, and large sheets can be made up that remain quite stable. One of the joys of this material is that it is solid pine.

Timber
Make sure you know just what you need when you visit your timber merchant. There is a huge variety of beautiful timber to choose from, including eye-catching decorative pieces.

My favourite timber merchant in the UK is Richard Burbidge, as they supply a superb range of mouldings, carvings for decoration, hand rails, newel posts and general timber. Shop around for your materials – look for a reputable timber merchant you can rely on, no matter what the job. Try looking in the telephone directory, ask in your local hardware store and even ask your friends and colleagues for recommendations. Once you have found a merchant you can trust, you will be confident to tackle all sorts of projects, knowing you can go to them for the necessary materials.

Don't expect the merchant to cut everything to length, but if you explain what you are doing and what it is you need, they are usually very helpful. A word of advice – don't go at busy times, when builders are setting up for a day's work. Wait until the rush is over, and you will get better service.

Water- and boil-proof plywood (WBP) is used by builders to make concrete shuttering, and when it is finished with, it is burnt. It is an external grade plywood, not as high quality as marine plywood – but then you are unlikely to want to sail your shredder store or compost bin! What all this means is that when the plywood gets wet, the layers of timber will not delaminate and fall to pieces. The very best grade of plywood is Finnish, and this is also reflected in the price, but the birch plywoods made by the Finns are lovely to work with.

I used shiplap boards for roofing the items. I have to say, I do like shiplap-board roofs; they look the part in the garden, and they make things a lot simpler than using roofing felt.

Timber merchants

Timber merchants are wonderful places to visit, but if you are not used to visiting a timber merchant, it is very easy to become somewhat overwhelmed by the huge variety of different timber sizes and shapes available. To make it easier, both for yourself and the timber merchant, be prepared. You should be clear about exactly what you need, so go armed with your cutting list (clear, easy-to-follow cutting lists are provided for every project in the book, so just take this along with you).

STUCK UP

Technology has not only changed the tools that we use, it has also come to our rescue in fixing things together permanently. Only recently, there was a glue pot in every carpenter's shop throughout the country. The pot sat on the old 'go-slow' stove and as it bubbled away, it gave off a pungent smell. The glue had to be used while hot, so gluing up was a bit of a furious job that entailed a lot of rushing around. Today, glues are sophisticated, and targeted at specific materials and applications. Wood, metal, fibreglass, leather, perspex, glass – there is a glue to suit you and your project. It also dries (cures) very quickly, otherwise we could not finish some of these projects in just a weekend.

Over the years, glues have increased in strength and some are now stronger than the material they fasten together. Wood has lots of fibres, which absorb some of the glue and so create a good bond between the sections of timber. It is worth taking two lengths of timber and doing an experiment to see just how strong the glue you are using is. Glue both timbers together, clamp them lightly and allow the glue to cure (the glue needs to be in a warm workshop to cure rapidly). Remove the clamp and try separating the timbers – you can break the timber, but not the joint. Examine it carefully and you will see that the timber fibres have given way, but not the joint.

In a woodworking projects book of this nature, glue is an important factor in creating rigidity in the items. Nowadays cabinetmakers join timber using some very traditional and functional joints, held together with glue and with absolutely no nails or screws in sight. This book is not intended for such craftmasters. The items made here need to look good and, let's face it, not everyone is proficient at cutting dovetail joints, so we require both screws and glue to hold the joints rigidly together.

UHU has a wide range of glues, but for my projects, I have used a great deal of the UHU Universal Wood Glue. This is water-resistant, and therefore perfect for these projects, all of which will be subject to the damp. It is not intended for immersion in water, so provided that you do not want to float your garden seat among the water lilies, all will be well.

If the timber to be jointed has previously been planed, then it is a good idea to roughen it up a little before you begin gluing. I use a Stanley knife and make a series of hash cuts into the timber. This allows a greater gluing area and, very importantly, an even stronger joint.

Special Glues
WOODTITE

You may find that the joint between two pieces of wood is occasionally a bit 'gappy'. UHU has developed a special product for just such an occasion. Called 'Woodtite', it not only holds the timber together, but also fills the gap. I also found it very useful when mending Windsor chair rails. Clean the joint out, apply Woodtite, and you produce a solid joint.

EPOXY

Epoxy glues have been around for while – most of us have used them. They are very strong and the glued joint will last for several years. With this sort of glue you also get a hardener, and it is important that you mix together equal quantities of each one. Measuring the correct amounts of a small squirt of epoxy glue and its hardener has always been a bit of a fiddly, hit-and-miss business.

Now, UHU has developed a 'combination' tube (container), making the job so much easier. The glue comes in a double pack with twin nozzle ends, and depressing a tube plunger releases equal quantities of glue and hardener. There are two choices of glue – heavy duty (for sticking the house together) and a fast-setting variety.

HOT-MELT GLUE GUNS

These electrically-operated glue guns are light years ahead of the old carpenter's hot glue pot. Inside the gun is an electric element that hot-melts the glue and feeds it onto the joint as you squeeze the trigger.

Now a word of warning here – the glue is boiling and if you get it on your fingers,

Wood glue
An indispensable part of your tool kit for the projects in this book. Well-glued joints are actually stronger than the timber itself.

it will burn. Speed is important, and once the glue has been applied, both surfaces need to be brought together rapidly.

Hot-melt glue guns are very useful as it sticks not just wooden joints but, by changing the glue stick to a multi-purpose glue, will do a variety of jobs around the house. Once you get used to the speed required to assemble the glued parts with these electric hot-melt guns, you will find many uses for them. But remember – keep your hands away from the glue!

OTHERS

UHU also makes glues for other applications: for instance, cans of carpet-fixing 'spray-on' glue and glues to stick your shoes together. The company has produced a useful glue tables chart on which you can cross-reference the different glues and find which type of glue is most suitable for your particular job.

Ten Rules for Perfect Adhesion

1. Always follow the directions for use
2. Clean thoroughly the surfaces to be glued. Remove rust and any remnants of paint, varnish or other material. Remove any grease with acetone, alcohol or white spirit. After cleaning, do not touch surfaces with your fingers. Roughen smooth surfaces with glasspaper (sandpaper)
3. Allow surfaces to dry
4. Apply adhesive thinly and evenly
5. When using contact adhesives, always observe open time
6. Ensure that the surfaces treated with adhesive remain clean and free from dust or dirt at all times
7. Always ensure that the surfaces to be glued are positioned correctly
8. Always pay attention to the drying time of the adhesive
9. If you are concerned about any adverse effect on the material to be glued, try the glue on a small sample first
10. Always remove excess adhesive immediately

WOOD CARE

When I make something, I like to get a good finish on it: I think that you can spoil a project by not achieving a good finish. The projects in this book have all been treated with Ronseal woodstains. This company produces a huge range of wood-care products to stop the ravages of rain, snow and frost destroying all your hard work. Not only does this protect your timber, but they dry very quickly – in ideal conditions in about an hour – so you can make the project in a weekend and apply your chosen finish.

I am one of those people who like to test the claims of manufacturers whenever possible, so when it is claimed that the woodstain will last for five years, I try it out. In that period of time, the available colours will change and the artwork on the tin will alter – but how does the woodstain live up to the claim?

One of my favourite tests is to make up a planter box, use the woodstain as recommended, fill the box with a layer of gravel, then compost or peat and then add plants. This is a severe test for a woodstain that is just brushed on to timber and not pressure-applied. The inside of the box is wet most of the time, and the box gets the full heat of the sun in summer and the destructive forces of frost in the winter. Thus my 'field tests' are tough – no pretty moisture-controlled laboratories, just the great big outdoors. And the results have been good. Planter boxes do not rot, and in spite of the sun and frost creating expansion and contraction of the timber, the woodstain is tenacious and sticks to the wood remarkably well. And over the years my planter box tests have shown that, in fact, the preserved timbers lasted well in excess of the manufacturer's own claims.

Therefore, it is a case of deciding exactly what degree of protection you want, for what particular project. I would not use the Ronseal five-year product on a trellis, but instead would choose the low-maintenance wood finish, because the solid colour is better for covering the lesser grade of timber I generally use for trellis. It will

20

also hide blemishes, so old timbers can be used, and made to look cared for, and the life expectancy of timber treated with this product is up to ten years. Ronseal produces a range of booklets giving the fullest information on its products and where and when they should be used. Once the correct product has been chosen, it is safe to leave it out in the garden, where you can enjoy the fruits of your hard work all year round.

ROT SPOTS

I have tried to design all the projects so that they will drain off after the rain and do not have corners where damp clings and encourages wood-rotting fungi or algae to stick to the timber. It is in the permanent damp spots that deterioration begins. In the case of the Compost Bin (page 66) and the Shredder Store (page 90), I have designed feet to keep the 'boxes' off the ground. This allows the air access to circulate and dry off the boards. And where timber is constantly in contact with the ground, such as with the Bridge (page 78), Bench (page 60) and Swing Seat (page 54), I have added separate battens of timber. As the feet are damp

most of the time, they will begin to rot, but it is a very simple job to remove them and screw new feet in place when necessary. The rest of the structure, raised above the ground, should remain intact and free of any rot.

Timber is quite good at shedding water, but the big problem starts when it cannot dry off. In many of the projects, I have mentioned Nordic spruce, which is very resistant to water and damp, so is always a good choice for garden furniture.

GARDEN FURNITURE MOT TEST

It pays at the beginning of spring to check all your garden furniture and, if there is a need for care and attention, to treat it immediately. The place I normally find decay starting is in the timber knots. The knot usually leaves an indentation in the wood, water gathers there, and before long rot sets in. Ronseal has a repair kit for this – in fact, the company has several approaches to this type of problem.

The first approach is to scrape out the knot area and remove all the decayed fibres. Then brush some 'wet-rot hardener' into the cavity. Once this has dried off, apply Ronseal filler, leaving it slightly proud so that you can sand it down to the level of the existing timber (this way you disguise the repair neatly).

Finish off the timber with your choice of woodstain. Finally, to prevent this type of decay ever happening again, bore a number of holes into the wood and insert Ronseal wet-rot tablets – that should fix the problem for ever.

Wood care
Just a few of the wood-care stains, varnishes, hardeners and fillers available in the wide range from Ronseal. A complete set of brochures is available from Ronseal on all their products; they make for a good read and will leave you well informed.

ADVANTAGES OF RONSEAL PRODUCTS

Ronseal's woodstains have a number of distinct advantages:

- They are easy to apply and very forgiving – if you get a dribble or two, you can brush them out
- They need no primers or base coats
- They are completely rainproof in only 30 minutes
- They are harmless to plants and animals. This means that there are no chemicals that will leach out into the soil
- The brushes can be cleaned in water
- It has no smell
- They stick to hardwood, softwood, planed timber and rough sawn
- They contain an ingredient that resists algae and surface mould

ALL THE COLOURS OF THE RAINBOW

Many years ago, I learnt the importance of using timber that was being grown from a source that was being replenished faster than it was being cut. The Nordic countries plant more trees than they fell, so I use Nordic red and white pine almost exclusively. The only exception to this is my use of Canadian white cedar, shipped over to me by the Quebec government. This source is also very carefully controlled, and timber cannot be felled in Quebec without the necessary licence, which is only provided after some very strict ground checks have been made by a very active inspectorate. There is no justifiable alternative to this approach, but it does mean that the projects can look a little bland when they are finished, as Nordic spruce and Quebec white cedar lack a strong grain and distinctive colour of their own.

I really do enjoy trying out some of the Ronseal Garden Woodstain colours. There are twelve in the range. Bilberry is a soft colouring, used on the

Roofed Garden Table (page 114). Harvest Gold, Evergreen and Terracotta were used on the Bridge (page 78). I think this mix and match of colours is good fun, and it certainly brings a real splash of colour to any winter garden. Jade Mist is another lovely colour, looking cool in the summer and cheerful in the winter.

All in all it is a case of get in there with the brushes, be bold, have a mix of colours – you really will not regret it. I first used this particular woodstain two years ago and there is absolutely no sign of deterioration in the timber projects or the finishes.

Old Garden Furniture

Sometimes the colours of old weather-worn furniture, fences and gates look a bit tired and the timber wants 'feeding'. Ronseal Low-Maintenance Wood Finish is perfect for this job. It has a low-sheen finish that waterproofs the timber and makes it look cared for. I used the Deep Mahogany on my twelve-year-old garden pergola and it has looked good throughout the winter. The finish has a 'solid' colour formula that hides blemishes and helps to repair the ravages of rain and snow. Its other great advantage is that it can be used over existing paint.

The Natural Beauty of Wood

For interior projects, there is an equally stunning range of finishes. On the Indoor Pebble Pool (page 38), I wanted to show off the carved embellishments and mouldings, so I used Ronseal's ultra-tough Satincoat Varnish – a couple of coats produce a magnificent finish. This product is water-resistant, and as it is the pebbles that get the constant soaking, not the wood, it is a good varnish for this job.

Brush Off

I know that it sounds very obvious, but you will not do the job justice if you use poor quality brushes. Stanley actually produces sets of professional brushes, which are not cheap, but will make a great difference to the finished article.

OUTDOOR TABLE

Eating out in the garden is one of the pleasures of the summer and early autumn. This table is designed with a generous top, but uses a central post leg to reduce its overall weight and the quantity of timber required. The feet are finished with small blocks to keep their undersides off the ground, which cuts down on rotting. The blocks also make it easier to get the table level on an outdoor surface. The table's other great advantage is that it can be made without traditional joints. All in all, it can be fairly described as a weekend project.

24

Dimensions

Height	32in (813mm)
Length	47in (1194mm)
Width	24in (610mm)

Tools

Pencil, expanding rule, carpenter's square, Jetcut saw, Bosch jigsaw (ideally use the 'Progressor' blade, which gives a superb finish), small hammer, Bosch battery drill/screwdriver, drill bits, countersink, hand plane, surform tool, Bosch random orbital sander.

Sundries

Zinc-plated screws (1¹/₂in/38mm, No. 8), wood adhesive, wood-care product.

Timber

Nordic red pine looks really good for this project. Make sure you select a knot-free post for the leg. Use mouldings for decoration as required.

Tip – Spacer Batten

When you have a lot of slats or battens to fix, such as with the table top, it is a good idea to make a spacer batten. Calculate the gap between the battens, and then cut a batten to the same dimensions. This will speed up the job because you can slot it between each slat as you fix them, saving you the need to measure each space.

Cutting List

LEGS AND FEET

Central post leg	1	31 x 2⁷/₈ x 2⁷/₈in (787 x 73 x73mm)
Shaped feet	2	22 x 4 x ⁷/₈in (559 x 102 x 22mm)
Shaped feet	2	12 x 4 x ⁷/₈in (305 x 102 x 22mm)
Feet blocks	4	4 x 2¹/₄ x ⁷/₈in (102 x 57 x 22mm)

TABLE TOP

Frame ends	2	22 x 3³/₄ x ⁷/₈in (559 x 95 x 22mm)
Frame sides	2	36 x 3³/₄ x ⁷/₈in (914 x 95 x 22mm)
Table slats	6	47 x 3³/₄ x ⁷/₈in (1194 x 95 x 22mm)

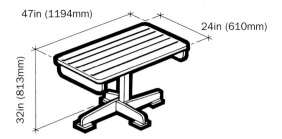

47in (1194mm)

24in (610mm)

32in (813mm)

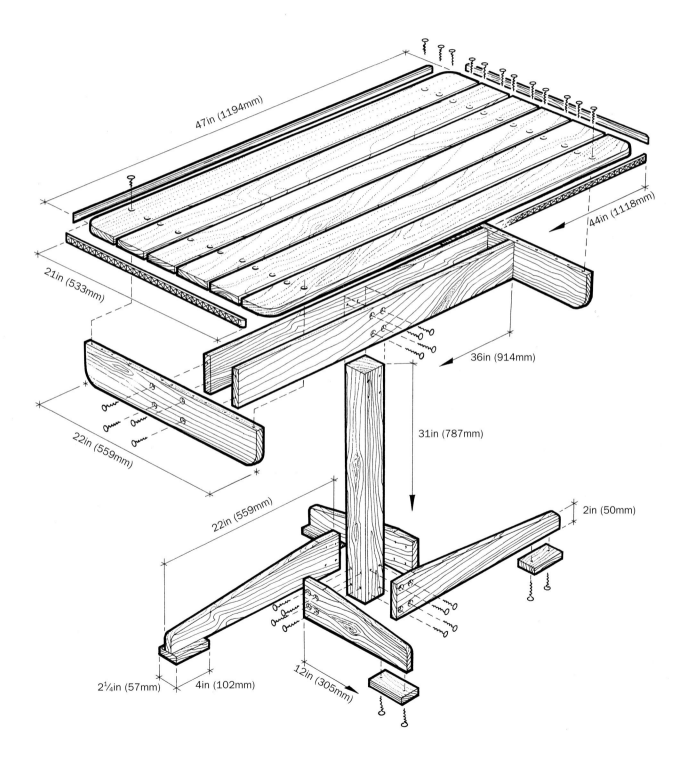

47in (1194mm)

44in (1118mm)

21in (533mm)

36in (914mm)

22in (559mm)

31in (787mm)

22in (559mm)

2in (50mm)

2¼in (57mm)

4in (102mm)

12in (305mm)

Construction

LEGS AND FEET

1 Cut the central post leg to length. Now cut the four feet. Following the diagram, pencil in the shape of each foot, and mark the position of the screw holes.

2 Take one marked-up foot, clamp it firmly to the bench and use a fine-cut blade in your jigsaw to cut out the desired shape. Repeat for the other three feet.

3 The small protective blocks are now glued and screwed onto each foot.

4 Now fit the feet to the central post leg. This is easier if you put the leg in a vice before starting work. Drill and countersink the screw holes in each foot. You can then start gluing and screwing each foot in place. As the job starts, it might resemble a signpost, but this soon gives way to a well-balanced table base.

TABLE TOP

1 The table top is fixed to a frame, which is now made and fitted. Cut the frame pieces to length. From the diagram you will see that the end pieces need to have a gentle curve cut on them before assembly.

2 Mark the positions of the screws in the centre of the long sides of the frame. Drill and countersink the holes, before gluing and screwing them to the central leg.

3 Mark the positions of the screws in the shaped frame ends, then drill and countersink the holes before attaching them to the frame sides.

4 Cut to length the six slats that form the top. It is very important that you cut the slats to exactly the same length, otherwise you will be unable to fix the mouldings to the ends (see step 6). You will see from the diagram that the slats on the outer edges need to have a radius cut on them. Do this now, using the jigsaw.

5 Screw the outer table top slats to the frame beneath, drilling and countersinking the necessary holes. The spacing between each slat is best achieved by making up a 'spacer' batten (see page 24) to exactly the right width, rather than measuring each gap individually.

Make sure that you line up all the slats at their ends before you start screwing them into place. It helps if you have a number of clamps to hold everything still before final fixing.

6 The lengths of moulding glued around the sides of the table top are optional, but do make it look well finished. You do not need to bend the moulding around the corners, just chamfer each end – it will look fine.

FINISH

Use a wood-care product as described on page 19. Here I have used Ronseal Quick-Drying Garden Woodstain in Jade Mist, which livens up a winter garden.

OUTDOOR STOOL

The traditional method of making stools would require the DIYer to have knowledge of how to cut mortice-and-tenon joints for the legs and rails. This project is a clear demonstration of how new technologies (*ie* glue and screws) have made it possible for everybody to have a go at garden woodwork. These little stools are the product of several years of on-going development. They are sturdy and very simple to make, having no traditional joints. Their design has another advantage: if you should wish to make several of them, say six, this is quite easy to do.

The stools are intended to complement the outdoor table (pages 22–26). If you prefer a bit of comfort, then a cushion should keep you sitting pretty.

Dimensions

Height   19in (483mm)
Length   20in (508mm)
Width   12¾in (324mm)

Tools

Pencil, expanding rule, carpenter's square, Jetcut saw, Bosch battery drill/screwdriver, drill bits, countersink, small hammer, and a Bosch random orbital sander.

Sundries

Zinc-plated screws (1½in/38mm, No. 8), wood glue, wood-care product.

Timber

Nordic red pine will do well for this project. You can use spruce for the legs, but it is not ideal for the top slats because its resin has a habit of oozing out. Use moulding for decoration as required.

Cutting List

Legs	4	18 x 2 x 1in (457 x 50 x 25mm)
Bottom side rails	2	17 x 2 x 1in (432 x 50 x 25mm)
Bottom end rails	2	12¾ x 2 x 1in (324 x 50 x 25mm)
Top side rails	2	17 x 3¾ x 1in (432 x 95 x 25mm)
Top end rails	2	12¾ x 3¾ x 1in (324 x 95 x 25mm)
Seat slats	5	12¾ x 3¾ x ⅞in (324 x 95 x 22mm)

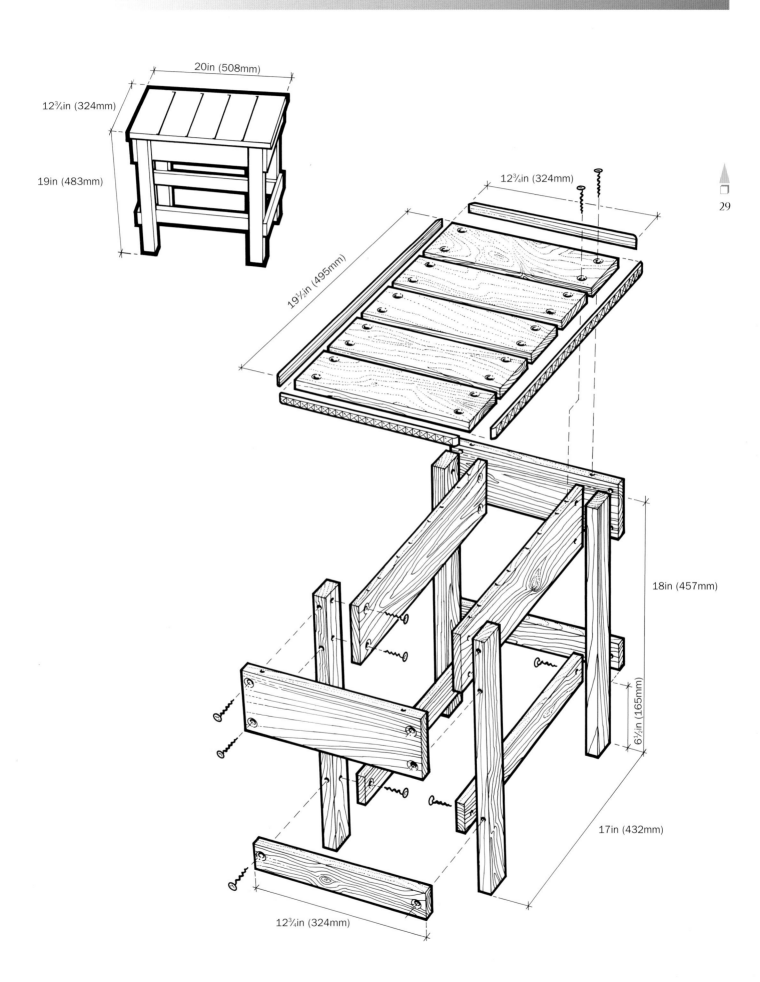

20in (508mm)

12¾in (324mm)

19in (483mm)

12¾in (324mm)

19½in (495mm)

18in (457mm)

6½in (165mm)

17in (432mm)

12¾in (324mm)

Construction

1 Make a start by cutting the four legs to length, followed by all the necessary rails for the sides and ends.

2 Following the diagram, position a pair of legs at the ends of a top and bottom side rail (effectively making up a side). Pencil in the position of the legs on the rails. Now mark the positions for the screw holes on the rails.

3 Bore and countersink the screw holes in the rails, then glue and screw one side of the stool together. When you position a leg on a rail, the glue in the joint will tend to make the parts move slightly, so screw carefully, and keep checking that the leg is at 90 degrees to the rail, and that the end of the rail is flush with the side of the leg.

4 Repeat steps 2 and 3 to construct the second side.

5 Fit the end rails to the sides. It is far easier to do the drilling and countersinking on the workbench before offering up the rails to be screwed. At this point, an extra pair of hands will be very useful – someone to hold the two sides while you glue and screw the end rails in place.

6 Once the glue has cured, and that does not take long, work over the legs and rails with glasspaper in order to remove any sharp edges.

7 Prepare the five slats that form the seat by drilling and countersinking the screw holes that hold them to the stool top. Remove the squareness of the outer slat edges by running a smoothing plane down them.

8 Now glue and screw the slats to the stool. Use a spacer batten as described on page 24. As this is something that will be sat on, make sure that all the screws are driven well into all the countersunk holes.

9 Moulded strips can be added to enhance the stools.

10 It is a good idea to finish off by just running a Bosch random orbital sander over the seat to ensure that the surface is ultra smooth.

FINISH
Use a wood-care product as described on page 19. Here, I have used Ronseal Quick-Drying Garden Woodstain in Jade Mist, to match the table (page 26).

TWO-TIER FLOWER CRADLE

Planting boxes in which to show off plants and flowers are always in demand. Conscious of the space that conventional boxes take up, I have designed this one with two tiers. The boxes themselves can be as plain or elaborate as you wish. For my design, I used decorative strip mouldings and carved embellishments as I wanted the cradle to occupy a central place in the conservatory. A wide variety of mouldings is readily available in big DIY stores, so individualizing your flower cradle is easy.

This is not a vastly difficult project to make, but you will need to use a jigsaw to achieve the gentle curve in the box front.

Dimensions

Height   36½in (927mm)
Width   42¾in (1086mm)
Depth   8in (203mm)

Tools

Pencil, expanding rule, sliding
bevel gauge, Jetcut saw, Bosch
battery drill/screwdriver, drill
bits, countersink, small hammer,
Bosch jigsaw, several small
cramps, smoothing plane,
bradawl, Stanley knife.

Sundries

Zinc-plated screws (2½in/63mm
No. 8 and 1½in/38mm, No. 8),
wood glue, wood-care product.

Timber

Very wide spruce planks are ideal
for this sort of box because they
withstand the damp very well.
Tongue-and-groove floorboards
are used for the bases of the
boxes. Mouldings for decoration
as required.

Cutting List

BOTTOM BOX

Base T & G board	2	34½ x 5½ x ⅞in (876 x 140 x 22mm)
Front and back	2	39 x 10½ x ⅞in (991 x 267 x 22mm)
Back top (for shaping)	1	39 x 11¼ x ⅞in (991 x 286 x 22mm)
Side	2	14½ x 10½ x ⅞in (368 x 267 x 22mm)
Feet	4	11 x 2¾ x 1½in (279 x 70 x 38mm)

TOP BOX

Base T & G board	2	22¾ x 5½ x ⅞in (578 x 140 x 22mm)
Front and back	2	25 x 7 x ⅞in (635 x 178 x 22mm)
Side	2	10 x 8 x ⅞in (254 x 203 x 22mm)
Upright posts	2	27 x 2 x 2in (584 x 50 x 50mm)

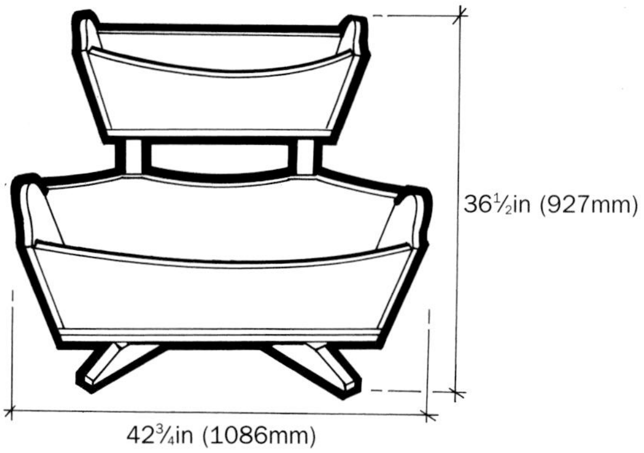

36½in (927mm)

42¾in (1086mm)

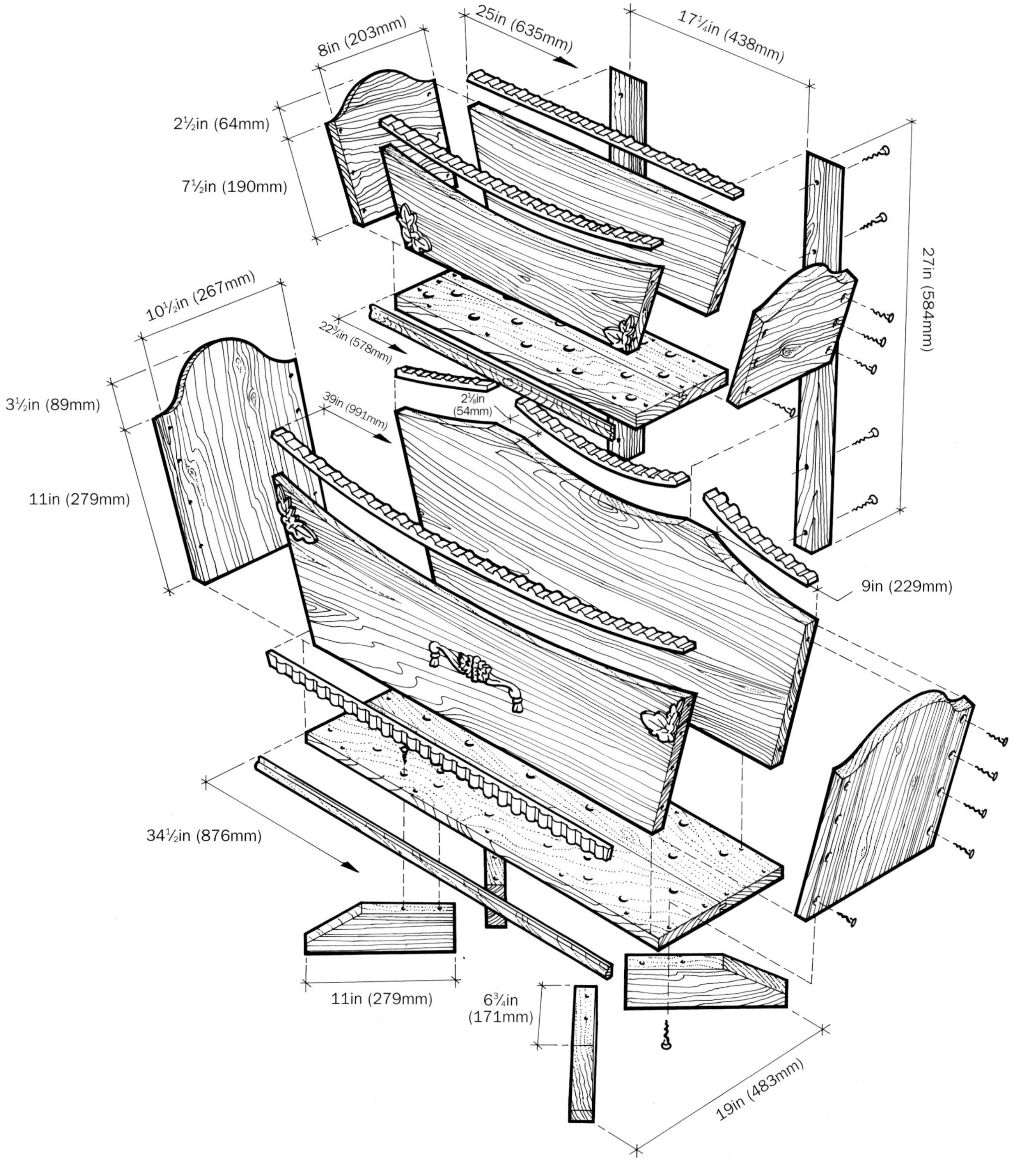

8in (203mm)

25in (635mm)

17¼in (438mm)

2½in (64mm)

7½in (190mm)

27in (584mm)

10½in (267mm)

22¾in (578mm)

3½in (89mm)

39in (991mm)

2⅛in
(54mm)

11in (279mm)

9in (229mm)

34½in (876mm)

11in (279mm)

6¾in
(171mm)

19in (483mm)

Construction
LARGE BOX

1 The starting place for this project is the base. When you cut the tongue-and-groove boards to length, remove the groove on one piece and the tongue from the other, so that the two outside edges of the planks are flat. Like this the two boards provide a strong base.

2 Now mark out the front, back and sides, using the diagram to draw in the angles, ideally using a sliding bevel gauge. Cut these angles very carefully with a Jetcut saw – the fine-toothed variety is best for all these jobs.

3 Mark the long, gentle curve on the front of the box. You can do this with a pencil tied to a length of cord as a trammel, but the most effective method is to use a thin batten. First mark a centre point on the plank and then flex the batten to form a curve. The centre point indicates the bottom of the curve. Practise flexing the batten, and once you are confident, get a helper to pencil a line along the curve it has made. This method is simple and gives a good clean curve.

4 Now clamp the front of the box to your workbench and jigsaw along the pencil line. Do not forget to wear safety specs. The Bosch Progressor blade is perfect for this job. Its teeth are made to cut wood very cleanly and to leave practically no marks. Normally after jigsawing there is a fair bit of work to do 'cleaning off' the saw teeth marks, but this new blade is really something special – try it!

5 Use the same technique as described in step 3 to mark up the curves on the section of timber for the back of the box. Once again the jigsaw is used to cut out the curves. Once the timber is shaped, glue it on to the top edge of the back. To add strength to the glued joint use a Stanley knife to cut along the edges of both pieces. Apply glue to the joint, and literally rub one piece against the other to make sure of a good bonding. Wipe off any excess glue with a cloth, and allow to dry.

6 The ends are now cut and shaped. It is probably simplest to make a cardboard template for this job. Pencil in the shape on card, cut it out with scissors, and transfer it on to the timber. Make sure the timber is firmly clamped to the bench before you start to cut. Keep it well on the bench, with as little protruding over the edge of the bench as possible, otherwise the timber will vibrate. You may have to stop and readjust the timber as the cut progresses – this is quite normal. Cutting the wood is not a problem, but holding it firmly is more difficult.

7 Bore and countersink the screw holes in the end pieces.

8 Because of the angles on the front and back pieces, the bottom edges of the side pieces will need to be shaped. Assemble the box 'dry' so that you can see the small angle that needs to be planed off to get the sides to fit flush on the bottom.

9 Glue and screw the ends to the sides: this is done so that you do not see the screw holes from the front.

10 Now glue and screw the base on to the underside of the box. You must check that the box is square at this point. Hopefully the base, being oblong and having 'square' ends, will be a good guide. Use 2¹/₂in/63mm No. 8 screws for attaching the base to the box.

11 Cut all the feet. Mark one with the shape to be cut out, using the diagram as a guide. A smoothing plane is ideal for this job. Fix the foot firmly in the vice first. Once you have shaped up one foot, use it as a template for the others. There are small chamfers at the front edges of the feet, which can also be done with the plane. When all four feet are shaped, they can be screwed to the base.

12 I am told by my gardening friends that I do not make the holes in my boxes big enough, so this time, to keep them happy, let me suggest ³/₄in (20mm) holes. These can be bored using a flat bit, which is the least expensive of boring bits. Dot the holes randomly. It is far easier to drill these holes with the bottom planks fixed in place.

TOP BOX

1 Cut to length the two uprights that will hold the top box. Cut the top end at an angle to disperse water.

2 Now cut out and make the top box, following the steps for making the bottom box. You do not have to make feet, as the uprights hold the box aloft.

3 Once the top box is made, glue and screw the uprights to both boxes.

FINISH

Now for the mouldings, which can turn an ugly duckling into a swan. Do look carefully at all the mouldings available, particularly the carved floral ones. When you have made your choice, they need cutting to length and gluing to the boxes. You will need as many cramps as you can lay your hands on and, if possible, some packing tape.

Cut the mouldings to length. Using a Stanley knife, lightly hash the surface to be glued, and the surface it will glue on to. Position the mouldings. Use clamps to hold them in position on the curved sections, using packing tape as well to reinforce the hold. Be careful that the cramp heads do not mark the moulding – slip a piece of packing beneath if necessary. With large carved mouldings, it is simpler to keep them in place with panel pins. Pull the pins out once the glue has cured.

Use a wood-care product as described on page 19. Here I have used Ronseal Natural Shades Varnish in Lemonwood. If you are planning to put the planter outside, Garden Woodstain is a better choice.

INDOOR PEBBLE POOL

We all like our gardens, particularly water features, but for many of us the weather does not allow the outdoors to be enjoyed all year round. Therefore I devised this wooden container to house a pebble pool that can be set up indoors. If you have a conservatory or perhaps a large hallway, it will really be enhanced by the pool, and you can enjoy the sound of running water throughout the seasons.

I do not know who came up with the ingenious idea of a small quantity of water being recycled through a pump over rocks and stones – but it was certainly a brilliant one. The timber surround I have used is perfect for displaying plants and rocks, although it is surprising just how many stones are needed to cover up the pebble pool plastic cover.

Dimensions

Height   14¼in (362mm)
Length   33½in (851mm)
Width   33½in (851mm)

Design Tip

The pebble pump and moulded plastic unit on which I based my design were made by Hozelock. If you use a different unit you will have to measure it up yourself, and then cut your timber accordingly.

Tools

Pencil, expanding rule, carpenter's square, Jetcut saw, Bosch battery drill/screwdriver, drill bits, countersink, smoothing plane, mitre block and tenon saw (for professional mitres on the mouldings), hammer, pincers, clamps, Stanley knife.

Sundries

Pebble pool and pump (supplied as a unit), rocks, stones or pebbles. Screws (2in/50mm, No. 8 and 1½in/38mm, No. 8), wood glue, wood-care product.

Timber

Nordic red pine edge-laminated boards look best. The mouldings and carved embellishments are widely available, and come in a huge variety.

Cutting List

Sides	2	30¾ x 9½ x ¾in (781 x 241 x 19mm)
Ends	2	29¼ x 9½ x ¾in (743 x 241 x 19mm)
Base battens – side	2	32 x 1¾ x ⅞in (813 x 44 x 22mm)
Base battens – end	2	28½ x 1¾ x ⅞in (724 x 44 x 22mm)
Base batten – centre	1	28½ x 3¾ x ⅞in (724 x 95 x 22mm)
Top battens – side	2	32 x 3 x ⅞in (813 x 76 x 22mm)
Top battens – end	2	28½ x 3 x ⅞in (724 x 76 x 22mm)
Corner blocks	4	8 x 8 x ¾in (203 x 203 x 19mm)
Top sides	2	33½ x 3 x ⅞in (851 x 203 x 22mm)
Top ends	2	32 x 3 x ⅞in (813 x 203 x 22mm)
Side mouldings	2	33½in (851mm) as purchased
End mouldings	2	32in (813mm) as purchased

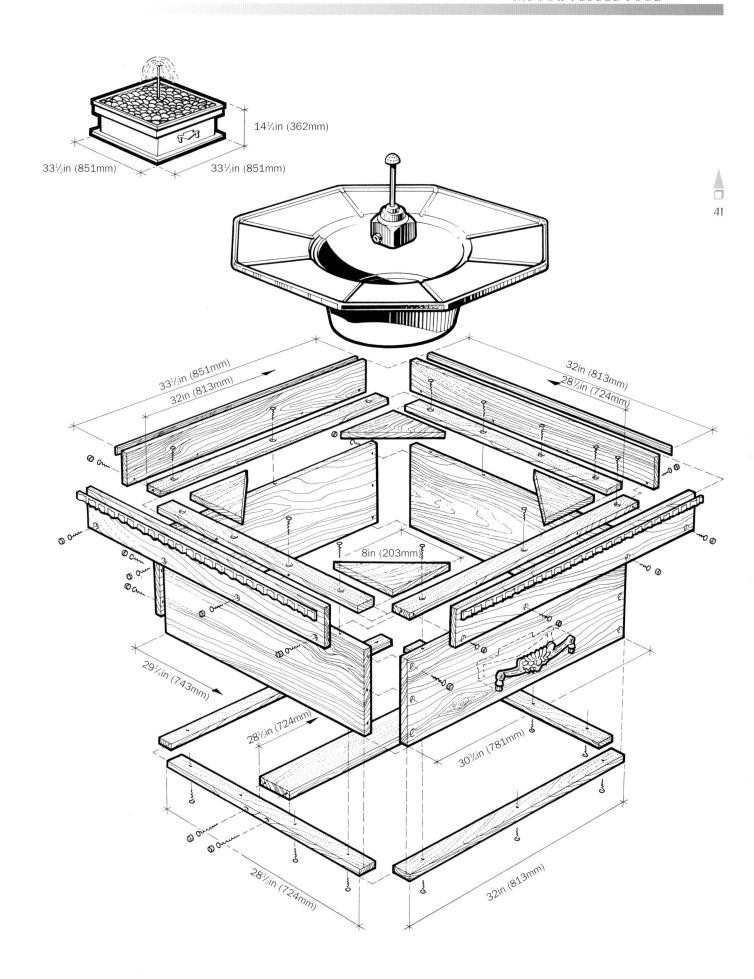

14¼in (362mm)

33½in (851mm)   33½in (851mm)

33½in (851mm)
32in (813mm)

32in (813mm)
28½in (724mm)

8in (203mm)

29¼in (743mm)

28½in (724mm)

30¾in (781mm)

28½in (724mm)

32in (813mm)

Construction

1 Mark up the pieces for the sides and ends. Use a Stanley knife to go over the pencil line before you cut the board. This is known as 'knifing in' and can be done on all four faces if you wish. Knifing in does two things: it gives the saw a line to follow, and it makes the cut edges very clean and sharp.

2 Glue and screw the pieces together to make a box. This is quite a big structure, so an extra pair of hands is helpful. If no volunteers are available, then glue and screw an end to a side to make an L-shape. Repeat for the other end and side. Then join the two 'Ls' together.

3 Now check that the box structure is square, using a thin batten that is about 2–3in (25–50mm) longer than the length of the boxes' diagonal. Press one end of the batten into one corner, and with a pencil make a 'tick' on the wood where the batten rests on the opposite corner. Remove the batten and check the other diagonals. If the 'tick' falls exactly on the second corner then the box is square. If not, then lean gently on a side before the glue sets, and you will be able to square the box up.

4 Cut the battens that go on to the base, not forgetting the central batten that provides the support for the pebble pool. Glue and screw these in place.

5 Battens are now screwed around the top edge. You can simply butt-joint them where they meet, or you can make mitre joints for a more professional finish. Stanley have made a mitre box with cam clamps inside for the smartest set of mitres you have ever had. You simply place the timber on the box, flick the cam clamps, and the timber is held tight while you cut. This simple device is just perfect for cutting mouldings.

6 Next you need to cut the triangular corner blocks (*see* diagram). These support the side lips of the plastic pebble pool. Use UHU glue to stick them in place.

7 You can now cut and fix the top side and end pieces, and set them off with the mouldings of your choice. All the mouldings are stuck on and held in place while the glue dries using panel pins. The big carved mouldings are also stuck on and held in place with panel pins. Be sure to use pincers to remove the pins once the glue has cured, otherwise someone will get a very nasty scratch.

FINISH
Use a wood-care product as described on page 19. Here I have used Ronseal Matt Varnish. It looks good, and it brings out the natural 'glow' in the timber.

Once it is dry, you can insert the pebble pool. Seal the lips of the pool to the wood using black mastic – this will prevent the water getting inside the box.

Be sure to follow the maker's instructions for setting up the electrics. The pump heads usually have a variety of different jets, which will need to be adjusted to suit. Be warned – it's a matter of getting wet to start with.

With the pump working it is time to arrange the small stones and pebbles in place. Finally, arrange some plants around the pool to complement the stones and rocks.

FOUR-TIER CORNER PLANT STAND

I have often thought that the idea of a corner cupboard could be applied to plant display, and so came up with this attractive yet simple design. Stocked with flowers and plants, it would look lovely in any corner of the garden, and equally good on a patio or terrace. The beauty of this unit is that it is fairly easy to construct, yet looks good no matter what the setting.

In order to get the necessary width of timber to make the shelves, I used edge-laminated pine boards. This material is so useful, and if you like working with solid timber, then it is just perfect.

Dimensions

Height   43½in (1105mm)
Width   25in (635mm)

Tools

Pencil, expanding rule, Jetcut saw, Bosch battery drill/screwdriver, drill bits, countersink and wooden plug cutter, small hammer, Bosch jigsaw and 'Progressor' blade, router with cutter to form the shelf edge (the router cutter requires a ball bearing on the end to guide the tool).

Sundries

Zinc-plated screws (1½in/38mm, No. 8), glue, wood-care product.

Timber

Nordic red pine for the central post and shelf supports. Red pine edge-laminated boards to form the shelves.

Cutting List

Vertical post	1	42¾ x 2 x 2in (1086 x 50 x 50mm)
Base support (back right)	1	16½ x 3¾ x ⅞in (419 x 95 x 22mm)
Base support (back left)	1	15½ x 3¾ x ⅞in (394 x 95 x 22mm)
Base support (front right)	1	11⅜ x 3¾ x ⅞in (389 x 95 x 22mm)
Base support (front left)	1	11 x 3¾ x ⅞in (279 x 95 x 22mm)
Bottom shelf support (right)	1	14¾ x 3¾ x ⅞in (375 x 95 x 22mm)
Bottom shelf support (left)	1	13¾ x 3¾ x ⅞in (349 x 95 x 22mm)
Centre shelf support (right)	1	10¾ x 3¾ x ⅞in (273 x 95 x 22mm)
Centre shelf support (left)	1	9¾ x 3¾ x ⅞in (248 x 95 x 22mm)
Top shelf support (right)	1	9⅛ x 3¾ x ⅞in (232 x 95 x 22mm)
Top shelf support (left)	1	8⅛ x 3¾ x ⅞in (206 x 95 x 22mm)
Base	1	18 x 18 x ¾in (457 x 457 x 19mm)
Bottom shelf	1	15¼ x 15¼ x ¾in (387 x 387 x 19mm)
Centre shelf	1	11½ x 11½ x ¾in (292 x 292 x 19mm)
Top shelf	1	9½ x 9½ x ¾in (241 x 241 x 19mm)

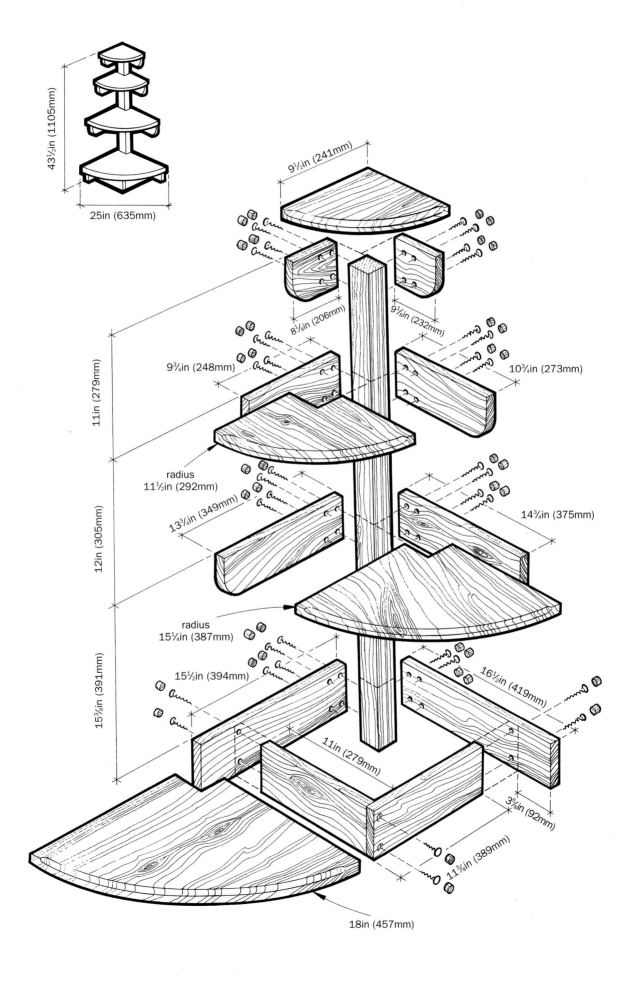

43½in (1105mm)

25in (635mm)

9½in (241mm)

8⅛in (206mm)

9⅛in (232mm)

11in (279mm)

9¾in (248mm)

10¾in (273mm)

radius
11½in (292mm)

13¾in (349mm)

14¾in (375mm)

12in (305mm)

radius
15¼in (387mm)

15½in (394mm)

16½in (419mm)

15⅜in (391mm)

11in (279mm)

3⅝in (92mm)

11⅜in (389mm)

18in (457mm)

Construction

1 Cut the vertical post to length. It is best to choose a piece of timber that is knot free for this piece.

2 Next cut out all the shelf supports, starting with the four supports at the base, which ensure that the stand cannot fall forwards. The method used here for jointing is to counter-bore screw holes then drive in wood plugs to hide the screw heads. Attach the two back supports to the post first, then attach the two front supports to each other, before screwing them to the back supports. Be sure to check that they are all actually at 90 degrees to the ground.

3 The other shelf supports are now shaped up. Pencil in a gentle curve on the end of one, and cut to shape using a jigsaw. Use this as a template to do all the rest. They need to be cut individually, though, and not as a batch.

4 Glue and screw each pair of shelf supports to the post, using the diagram as a guide for positioning. Keep a constant check that each shelf support is at 90 degrees to the post.

5 With all the shelf supports in place, fit and glue wood plugs into all the counter-bored holes. Any excess can be trimmed off using a chisel.

6 Now the four shelves need to be cut. The best way to do this is to cut squares off a plank and then mark the semi-circle on the front edge of each. Mark the semi-circle using a paper or card template or make a trammel with a pencil, string and nail.

Whatever the method you use – remember to measure twice and cut once.

7 Use a fine blade (such as the Bosch 'Progressor') to cut each semi-circle. Also mark and cut out a square in the back of each shelf to allow it to fit neatly around the post. If you use the correct jigsaw blade, you will have no saw marks to clean off the curve.

8 By far the simplest and, indeed, prettiest method of decorating the curved front of the shelf is to use a router. A vast number of different cutter profiles (shapes) are available. A decorative edge softens the edge and prevents it looking chunky. If this is your first time with a router, this project will enable you to appreciate just how simple they are to use.

9 I simply glued all the shelves to the supports. If any of them show a tendency to lift, use a cramp to hold them in place while the glue dries.

FINISH

Use a wood-care product as described on page 19. Here, I have used Ronseal Matt Varnish. It dries in an hour and gives a tough surface. I find that a varnish doesn't compete with the colour of the flowers on display.

CLEMATIS PLANTER

Even the barest of gardens or patios can be given a new lease of life with the right plants. While visiting an exhibition staged by the Society of Clematis Growers, I was struck by how they had transformed what is normally a very anonymous exhibition hall with this stunning plant. Clematis come in a wide variety of colours, and gave me the inspiration to design and build it a special planter to make the most of its beauty.

Dimensions

Height	72in (1829mm)
Width	30in (762mm)
Depth	18in (457mm)

Tools

Pencil, expanding rule, carpenter's square, protractor, Jetcut saw, Bosch battery drill/screwdriver, drill bits, countersink, smoothing plane, clamps.

Sundries

Zinc-plated screws (1½in/38mm, No. 8), glue, wood-care product.

Timber

This is one occasion when you get a lot of project for the money! Most good timber merchants keep a full stock of 50 x 25mm (2 x 1in) timber. If this size is not available, ask for roofing battens, which should be suitable. This project is built entirely from sawn, batten-size material. Sawn is less expensive than planed, and it is ideal for this job as its rough surface is perfect for the clematis tendrils to grip on to.

Cutting List

PLANTER

Angled side slats	18	15½ x 1½ x ¾in (394 x 38 x 19mm)
Straight side slats	20	16½ x 1½ x ¾in (419 x 38 x 19mm)
Base	8	15⅞ x 2 x 1in (403 x 50 x 25mm)
Frame uprights	4	24 x 2 x 1in (610 x 50 x 25mm)
Frame bottom cross-pieces	2	15¼ x 2 x 1in (387 x 50 x 25mm)
Frame top cross-pieces	2	20½ x 2 x 1in (520 x 50 x 25mm)
Planter capping	2	15⅞ x 1½ x ¾in (403 x 38 x 19mm)
Planter capping	2	17¼ x 2 x 1in (438 x 50 x 25mm)
Frame top cross-pieces	2	15⅞ x 2 x 1in (438 x 50 x 25mm)

TRELLIS

Cross-bars	14	22¼ x 1½ x ¾in (565 x 38 x 19mm)
Main uprights	4	48 x 1½ x ¾in (1219 x 38 x 19mm)
'V' sidebars	4	26¼ x 1½ x ¾in (667 x 38 x 19mm)

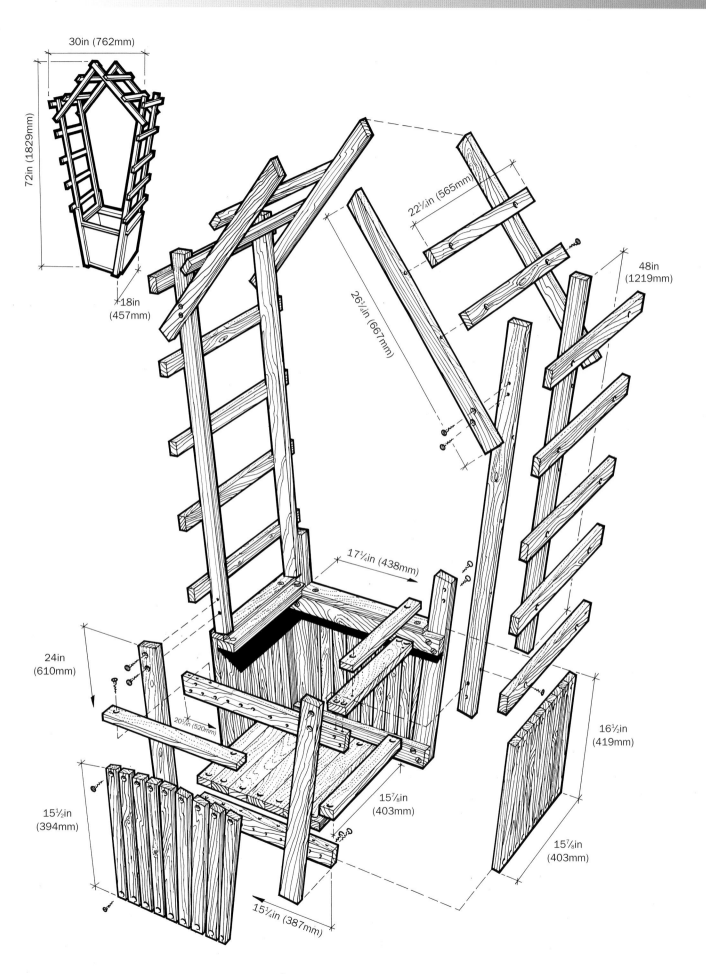

30in (762mm)

72in (1829mm)

18in (457mm)

22¼in (565mm)

48in (1219mm)

26¼in (667mm)

17¼in (438mm)

24in (610mm)

20½in (520mm)

16½in (419mm)

15⅞in (403mm)

15½in (394mm)

15⅞in (403mm)

15¼in (387mm)

Design Tip

Making square or rectangular shapes in timber is fairly simple, but when you introduce angles, a little more thought is required. Before you start this project, study the drawing carefully. The sides are parallel to each other while the two ends are angled, which sets the trellis off at a slant. This gives the planter its distinctive shape. It is a good idea to make a full side from cardboard, just to check that you are getting all the angles right.

Construction
PLANTER

1 Ideally using a full size paper or card template, mark the angles and cut the battens for the planter frame. Fit one pair of upright frame battens on the card template to check that the angles work, then drill and countersink the holes to take the screws in the 'top' timbers. Most screws in this project are fixed on the ends of the battens, so pre-boring is essential to avoid splitting the wood.

2 Arrange the two frame uprights back on the template then screw and glue the bottom frame cross-piece to them. Now do the same for the top frame cross-piece. This is the critical stage of setting the angle correctly.

3 Now make up the other end by lying the timbers over the first. In this way you ensure that both panels are the same.

4 Bore holes at each end of the eight base slats. Glue and screw these on to the top edge of both bottom cross-pieces of the frames you have already made. Space them out to allow for drainage. Now fit the two cross- pieces at the tops. Once this is done, you have formed the main 'box' framework.

5 Taking the 20 pieces of batten that form the sides, bore a hole in each end. Space 10 out along one side, leaving a small gap between each. When you are happy with the fit, glue and screw them in place. Repeat on the other side.

6 Now the angled front and back are constructed. Cut the 18 battens to length, nine for each end. The two outer battens of each end need to be shaped. It is almost a case of cutting a batten diagonally along its length, from one corner at the top to the opposite corner at the bottom. However, you will have to plane up these battens and must be prepared for a bit of trial and error to get a good fit.

7 Take one set of nine battens and check the fit on the template before boring holes in both ends of all of them. Find the centre of the front edge, and fix the middle batten in place on the bottom and top frame cross-pieces. Then glue and screw the others, working from the middle to the sides. It is best to position all the battens and check where the screws will go before you start gluing and fixing.

8 Repeat the checking and fixing process to assemble the other end of the planter.

9 The planter will look its best if you finish it by gluing and screwing capping battens along the top of all the panels. These battens will also prevent rain getting into the end grain of the panel tops.

TRELLIS

1 Cut the four main uprights to length, tape them together, and then pencil in the positions for the five trellis cross-pieces across all four.

2 Glue and screw the trellis together. Clamp and screw the trellises on to the top of the planter box.

3 Now cut the four pieces that make up the V-shaped arch. Tape them together and mark the positions for the two trellis cross-pieces. Then glue and screw them in place.

4 At the top of the 'V', the battens are screwed together at 90 degrees. It is essential to drill pilot holes to prevent splitting the batten, and care is required when you are driving the screws.

5 The 'V' section is now screwed on to the trellis uprights, forming the arch.

FINISH

Use a wood-care product as described on page 19. Here I have used Ronseal Low-Maintenance Wood Finish. This has a 'solid' finish that is particularly good on a surface such as roofing batten, which is a relatively low grade of timber.

SWING SEAT

A quiet garden, a shady corner, a good book and a garden swing seat – what could be better? There is something very therapeutic about swing seats, and they have that added advantage of a totally adjustable seat height – you can swing with your toes just touching the ground, or your feet in the air, depending on how the mood takes you, simply by hooking the chains up or down a link.

This swing seat, which seats two quite comfortably, is not difficult to put together because there is no need to make any traditional joints. It is made from either red or white pine, or from a combination of the two. Paint the seat in your favourite vivid colour, and this stylish and attractive piece of furniture is sure to enhance any area of the garden.

Dimensions

Height	76in (1930mm)
Width	68in (1727mm)
Depth	50in (1270mm)

Tools

Pencil, expanding rule, clamps, Stanley hand plane, drill, drill bits and countersink, Jetcut saw. A cordless screwdriver, an orbital sander and a jigsaw will speed up the work tremendously.

Sundries

Screws (1½in/38mm, No. 8), ³⁄₁₆in (5mm) galvanized steel rod (12 pieces, length to suit), nuts and washers, ³⁄₁₆in (5mm) eyebolts (six, length to suit), six shackles, chain (to suit purpose) UHU water-resistant wood adhesive, wood-care product.

Cutting List

FRAME

Leg	4	3 x 1½ x 76in (76 x 38 x 1930mm)
Side upper	2	3 x 1½ x 23in (76 x 38 x 584mm)
Side centre	2	3 x 1½ x 40in (76 x 38 x 1016mm)
Side lower	2	3 x 1½ x 48in (76 x 38 x 1219mm)
Arm rest	2	5 x 1 x 42in (127 x 25 x 1067mm)
Wide spacer: top front, top rear, lower rear	3	6 x 1 x 66in (152 x 25 x 1676mm)
Narrow spacer: rear	1	3 x 1 x 62in (76 x 25 x 1575mm)
Narrow spacer: under	1	3 x 1 x 65in (76 x 25 x 1651mm)
Seat support beam	1	3 x 1½ x 68in (76 x 38 x 1727mm)
Feet	4	3 x 1½ x 6in (76 x 38 x 152mm)

SWING SEAT

Shaped back former	3	3 x 1 x 30¼in (76 x 25 x 768mm)
Seat top cover piece	1	4 x 1 x 46in (101 x 25 x 1168mm)
Shaped seat former	4	3 x 1 x 18³⁄₈in (76 x 25 x 467mm)
Seat bottom cover piece	1	4 x 1 x 46in (101 x 25 x 1168mm)
Shaped top of seat	1	5 x 1 x 49in (127 x 25 x 1245mm)
Seat slats: back and seat	11	3 x 1 x 46in (76 x 25 x 1168mm)
Eyebolt mount	4	3 x 1 x 3in (76 x 25 x 76mm)

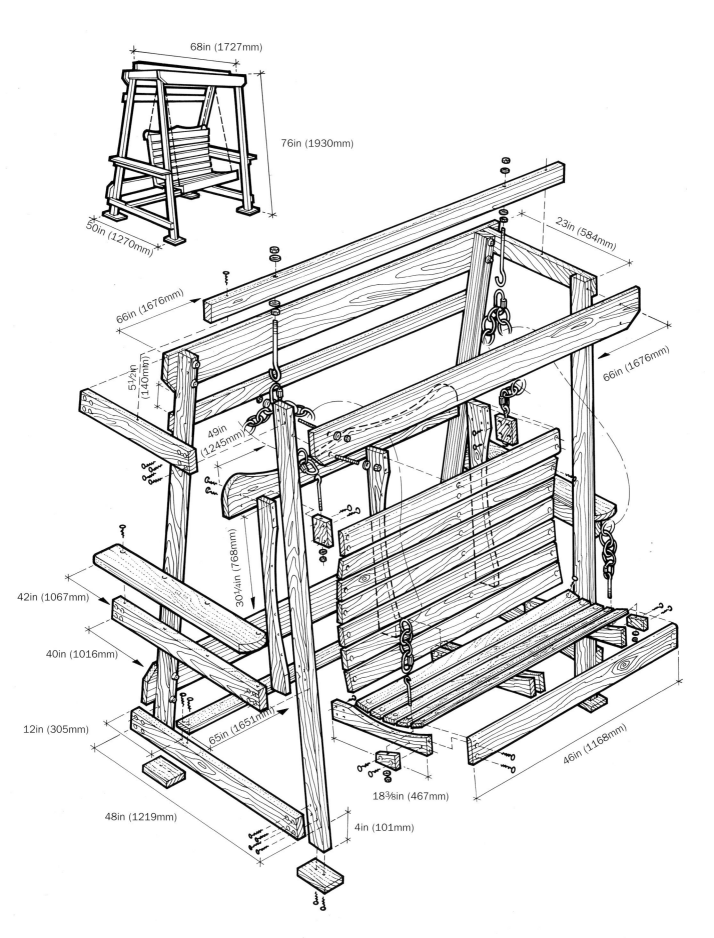

68in (1727mm)

76in (1930mm)

50in (1270mm)

23in (584mm)

66in (1676mm)

66in (1676mm)

5½in (140mm)

49in (1245mm)

30¼in (768mm)

42in (1067mm)

40in (1016mm)

12in (305mm)

65in (1651mm)

46in (1168mm)

18⅜in (467mm)

48in (1219mm)

4in (101mm)

Design Tips

Combining Nordic white spruce and Nordic red pine is a good idea. The legs and swing frame can be made in spruce, and red pine is best for the slatted seat as it has no resin pockets to damage your clothes.

To simplify the construction of the front and the back of the frame, I used pieces of threaded galvanized steel rod. This is available in metric lengths, and is also accompanied by packs of galvanized nuts and washers; this works out much cheaper than using coach bolts for the same purpose. Cut the rod to the lengths required.

Construction
THE FRAME

1 Make a start on the frame by cutting the four legs to length. As you can see from the diagram on page 57, you will need to cut the ends of the legs at a slight angle.

2 Now cut the six side battens (three per side) to size. In the same way as the legs, the battens have angled ends – these are cut after assembly.

3 Lay the legs on a flat surface – your workshop or garage floor will serve perfectly well for this. Separate the legs into pairs (one front and one back) and use a pencil to mark where the side battens will go on each pair.

4 It is always best to try things out with a dry run before you start the final assembly. Do this with one pair of legs (see step 6). Position the three battens in place, making sure they are lined up with the pencil marks. Use clamps to keep the battens still while you check the side frame carefully to see that all is well. If it is, disassemble the frame, removing the battens, bore four holes into each end of each of the battens, then remake the frame, gluing and screwing the battens onto the legs.

5 Remember that timber which has glue on it will tend to slide around, so watch out for this as you tighten the screws.

6 When the glue has dried on the first frame, assemble the second frame on top of it. This will ensure that you produce a matching pair.

7 When fitted to the centre batten, an armrest or shelf is an attractive addition to the swing seat. Use a jigsaw to cut it to any shape you like. Don't be tempted to leave square corners on the outside edges, as someone is bound to walk past and incur injury. Saw the corners off with the jigsaw, and use a sander to smooth the edges.

8 Cut the timbers that hold the two end frames together: three for the top and two for the base at the back. There are no timbers at the bottom front edge of the frame, as your feet would hit them as you swung to and fro; so I have made three of these timbers fairly substantial.

9 These timbers are joined by threaded galvanized steel rod (see Design Tip). Use clamps to hold the pieces of timber together, then drill holes that are slightly larger than the threaded steel rod. Push the pieces of threaded steel rod through the holes, and fix the whole lot together with washers and nuts.

10 The quality of the seat support beam is crucial. Select a piece of knot-free timber and bore the holes, following the diagram on page 57. The eyebolts that hold the chains will need a large washer beneath the nuts, in order to spread the weight and prevent them pulling through the holes when someone sits on the seat.

11 Once you have assembled the whole framework, check that everything lines up correctly before you tackle the job of making the swing seat itself.

THE SEAT

1 Study the diagram and you will see that the seat is made up of battens attached to wooden formers – three at the back and four at the base. The formers are made first (see below).

2 Following the diagram, use a jigsaw to cut a gentle curve in each of the formers. This will greatly add to the comfort of the seat when you sit on it. After sawing is complete, screw and glue the cover pieces to the formers to make the seat frame.

3 Cut the battens to be used to 'tie' the formers together and thus make the seat. It is a good idea to plane along the top edges of these battens – this removes any sharp edges. The batten that fits at the front (just where the back of your legs will go) needs particularly careful planing and sanding. Screw all the battens on to the formers. It's a good idea to find yourself a helper to hold things in place while the first battens are fixed.

4 To add a little style to the project, I used a jigsaw to shape up a section of timber for the top of the seat. You can make a paper template for this job, and transfer the shape on to the timber before cutting. Then screw this on to the back of the seat back formers.

5 Now you will need to make four blocks to create the seat anchorage points. However, it is best to buy the eyebolts first. Ideally, they need to be welded at the top. Cut the blocks to shape then drill a hole in each block, thread the eyebolt through, and then screw a large washer and nut onto the end. Now glue and screw the blocks on to the seat formers, as shown in the diagram.

6 Your local DIY store or builders' merchant will have a steel-link chain, and the screw shackles that join the chain and eyebolts together. Do not cut the chain to length at the outset – leave spare links. This also allows you to alter the height of the seat above the ground. You will find that rigging the seat and chain is best done with a helper as it is quite heavy work.

7 Because of the angle of the side frames, there is a small protruding 'triangular' piece to cut off on all the cross batten ends (see 'The Frame' step 2). Use a tenon saw and finish off with a very sharp Stanley smoothing plane.

8 As the garden swing will most likely stand on the lawn or garden patio, it is a good idea to make up four foot blocks, which are screwed on to the ends of the legs. These will be the first to suffer if any rot occurs at ground level, and they can easily be replaced, thus avoiding spoiling the legs of the frame.

FINISHING

Paint the garden swing seat in a Ronseal Garden Woodstain colour of your choice (see page 19). Here, I used Dark Blue.

GARDEN BENCH

Every garden ought to have a bench and, in my opinion, a comfortable two-seater is best. If you look at a really well-made park bench, there are lots of mortice and tenons and angular joints, and the whole thing has been made from some very lovely oak. But to keep it simple, the bench I have devised has no mortice and tenons, and is constructed from pine, so it is less expensive to make, too. Instead of the traditional joints, I have glued and screwed the pieces together, which makes a very rigid and solid bench. If you can use a saw, rule and powered screwdriver, then this project is a must for you.

Dimensions

Height	44in (1118mm)
Width	47in (1194mm)
Depth	22in (559mm)

Tools

Pencil, expanding rule, carpenter's square, Jetcut saw, clamps, Bosch battery drill/screwdriver, drill bits, countersink, smoothing plane, Magnum screwdrivers, Bosch jigsaw. If you want to cut some fancy moulded edges, then try the Bosch router.

Sundries

Zinc-plated screws (1½in/38mm, No. 8 and 3in/76mm, No. 8), glue, large sheets of paper, wood-care product.

Cutting List

Back legs	2	41¾ x 3½ x 1½in (1060 x 89 x 38mm)
Front legs	2	25 x 3½ x 1½in (635 x 89 x 38mm)
Side rail (top)	2	23 x 4 x 1½in (584 x 102 x 38mm)
Side rail (bottom)	2	20¼ x 6 x 1½in (514 x 152 x 38mm)
Under rails (back and front)	2	41½ x 3 x 1in (1054 x 76 x 25mm)
Seat back slats (above arm)	4	47 x 3 x 1in (1194 x 76 x 25mm)
Seat back slats (under arm)	2	44 x 3 x 1in (1118 x 76 x 25mm)
Seat slats (main)	5	44 x 3 x 1in (1118 x 76 x 25mm)
Seat slat (front)	1	41 x 3 x 1in (1041 x 76 x 25mm)
Bench front slat	1	44 x 3 x 1in (1118 x 76 x 25mm)
Feet	4	7 x 3 x 1in (178 x 76 x 25mm)
Arm rests	2	27½ x 3 x 1in (698 x 76 x 25mm)
Bench back top	1	47 x 3 x 1in (1194 x 76 x 25mm)

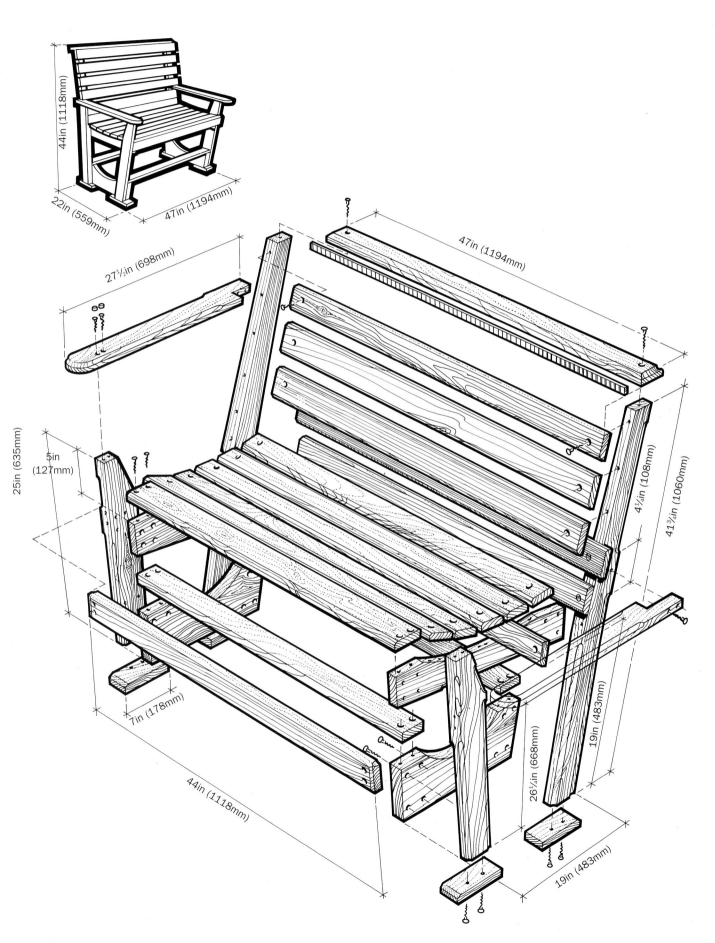

44in (1118mm)

22in (559mm)

47in (1194mm)

27½in (698mm)

47in (1194mm)

25in (635mm)

5in (127mm)

4¼in (108mm)

41¾in (1060mm)

7in (178mm)

19in (483mm)

26¼in (668mm)

19in (483mm)

44in (1118mm)

Design Tip

When you select timber, try to get the legs as knot free as possible, this being particularly important with the two back legs. It is best to work from the dimensions given and draw out the back leg full size on a couple of sheets of light card or paper before cutting it from the timber. In fact, it is helpful to draw out a full side, including the front leg and two connecting rails.

Construction

1 Having pencilled in the shape of the back leg on the piece of timber, fix it firmly to the bench and cut it to shape using a jigsaw and a fine-cut blade, such as the Bosch 'Progressor', which cuts cleanly and leaves no saw-tooth marks. When you use a jigsaw in fairly thick timber, as with this leg, it is important not to push it sideways, otherwise the blade will flex and the cut will not be parallel with the face of the work.

2 Use the first back leg as a template to mark up the second one, and cut this out in the same way. Repeat for the two front legs. The legs are decorated using a router, see step 6.

3 Now it is time to shape up the two pairs of side rails that hold the legs together. Both the rails are curved, the bottom one for appearance's sake, the top one for comfort. Use paper templates to sketch the curve, and then when satisfied, cut them out and transfer the shape on to the timber.

4 Firmly clamp one rail to the workbench, and then it's back to the jigsaw again. It is no more difficult to shape a curve than a straight line, just remember to feed the router steadily along

the timber. Repeat the operation for the other three rails.

5 Drill and countersink holes in the rails, before screwing and gluing them to the inside faces of the legs. Remember, once you have fixed the rails, there will be a left- and right-hand bench side.

6 It is at this stage that the shaping has to be done to the legs – it is too late once the arms and slats are attached. I used a router with a simple profile cutter that has a ball-bearing follower on the bottom. The ball bearing is the guide, and it also prevents the tip of the router coming into contact with the wood, which can result in burning. You steadily feed the router along the work, the cutter does the rest. You do need to mark in pencil the extent of the router cut, otherwise adjoining rails will not fit well.

7 Now cut all the slats and remaining rails to length. The seat and back slats will need some shaping to make them comfortable. You can plane off the 90-degree edge on each, or you can use a router to make a shape and thus remove the sharp edge. The two under rails (at the bottom of the bench) can also be given this treatment, but perhaps it is the slat at the front edge of the bench that needs the most careful rounding off, as this will fit into the back of your knees.

8 Cut out the arm rests, following the suggested shaping on the diagram and using a jigsaw. The edges of the arm rest can also be shaped using a router. Bosch not only make a pretty little machine, ideal for this sort of work, they also have a useful boxed set of router cutters, which gives you a choice of profiles.

9 Glue and screw the arm rests to the bench. I used a fairly lengthy 3in (76mm) screw at the front edge, as I wanted it to anchor itself well into the end grain. Benches are often lifted by their arm rests, and I did not want the embarrassment of mine coming off.

10 All the cross rails and slats (seat, back and bottom) are now glued and screwed in place. Start with the two under rails (back and front) and then add the seat slats. Use a spacer batten (*see* page 24) to drop between each slat as the fixing progresses; it saves you having to measure the gap each time. Not all the seat slats are identical in length (*see* cutting list). For example, the back slats are

longer than the seat slats, and the front seat slat fits between the two front legs, so is the shortest of all. Make sure you get them all in the right place.

11 I do like to add a slat on the top of the bench – it finishes the bench visually, and has an important task: it covers and also protects the end grain at the top of the legs. A further embellishment at the top is the addition of a small piece of moulding – the choice is yours.

12 End grain is always more vulnerable to wet than face grain, so shape up the four feet for the bottom of the legs, and glue and screw them into place. These four feet not only keep the bottom rails off the ground, but prevent the damp getting into the end grain.

FINISHING

Use a wood-care product as described on page 19. Here I have used Ronseal Garden Woodstain, which comes in nine colours – visualize the bench in position in the garden to help you choose one – Harvest Gold or Bilberry are good, or try Evergreen for the frame and Antique Pine for the seat slats. I find it helps to use a fairly small brush for applying the stain as there are lots of rails and slats to work around.

COMPOST BIN

We are all increasingly being encouraged to compost garden waste. It is fine to chop up branches and prunings, but it is equally important to put them somewhere, particularly lawn cuttings, the messiest thing in the garden – and a big composter is essential to cope with these.

This large-capacity composter is designed to do the job, and it also makes a matching pair with the Shredder Store (pages 90–95). You might like to double up the materials you buy and build both together. The work is practically identical, and it is quicker to do this than to come back to the Shredder Store job later on.

Dimensions

Height	49³/₄in (1264mm)
Width	29⁷/₈in (759mm)
Depth	25in (635mm)

Tools

Pencil, expanding rule, protractor, carpenter's square, Bosch drill/screwdriver (or equivalent), drill bits, countersink, Bosch circular saw, Jetcut saw, smoothing plane.

Sundries

Two T-strap hinges: 9in (229mm), two bolts, a pair of handles, zinc-plated screws (1¹/₂in/38mm, No. 8), black japanned round-headed screws (³/₄in/19mm, No. 8) for the hinges, glue, wood-care product.

Timber

The sides are made from one sheet of WBP plywood. The framing battens are standard 50 x 50mm (2 x 2in) Nordic spruce. The floorboards are tongue-and-groove Nordic spruce. Spruce withstands damp well, so is ideal as the bin will be in a permanently humid state.

Cutting List

Side panels (plywood)	2	48³/₄ x 25 x ³/₄in (1238 x 635 x 19mm)
Front (plywood)	1	40⁵/₈ x 24⁵/₈ x ³/₄in (1032 x 626 x 19mm)
Back (plywood)	1	48³/₄ x 24⁵/₈ x ³/₄in (1238 x 626 x 19mm)
Floor (T&G)	5	24 x 5¹/₂ x ⁷/₈in (610 x 140 x 22mm)
Feet	2	21 x 2 x 2in (533 x 50 x 50mm)
BIN FRAME		
Back battens	2	48³/₄ x 2 x 2in (1238 x 50 x 50mm)
Front battens	2	42 x 2 x 2in (1067 x 50 x 50mm)
Top battens	2	24⁵/₈ x 2 x 2in (626 x 50 x 50mm)
Bottom batten back	1	20¹/₂ x 2 x 2in (521 x 50 x 50mm)
Bottom battens side	2	23 x 2 x 2in (584 x 50 x 50mm)
Front hinge support batten	1	19¹/₂ x 3¹/₂ x 1in (495 x 89 x 25mm)
Roof shiplap	7	29⁷/₈ x 4¹/₂ x ⁵/₈in (759 x 114 x 16mm)
Roof side support battens	2	30³/₈ x 2³/₄ x ⁷/₈in (772 x 70 x 22)mm
Roof back support battens	2	24⁵/₈ x 2³/₄ x 1in (626 x 70 x 25mm)
Handle strengthener	2	11 x 3 x 1in (279 x 76 x 25mm)
Bolt keeper supports	2	5 x 2 x 2in (127 x 50 x 50mm)

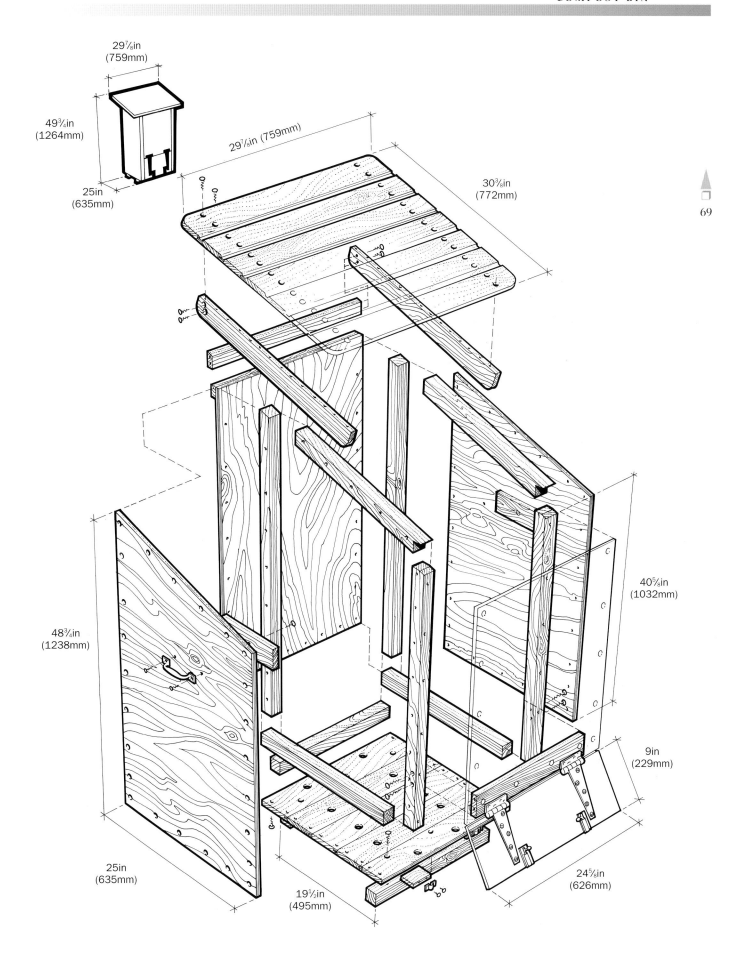

29⅞in
(759mm)

49¾in
(1264mm)

25in
(635mm)

29⅞in (759mm)

30⅜in
(772mm)

40⅝in
(1032mm)

48¾in
(1238mm)

9in
(229mm)

25in
(635mm)

19½in
(495mm)

24⅝in
(626mm)

Construction

BIN

1 Lay the plywood flat on the floor of your garage or somewhere similar, and mark out the panels before cutting. A mains-powered circular saw is the fastest and easiest tool to use because it is designed to cut straight lines. Make sure you wear safety specs. A big sheet of floppy plywood can be difficult to handle, so support it on a couple of lengths of 2 x 2in (50 x 50mm) timber, positioned either side of the line to be cut. In this way, as the cut progresses, the plywood does not 'pinch' the saw blade or stop it, which can be very dangerous with a circular saw.

If you don't have a circular saw, use a Jetcut saw, which will also do a very good job. Always make a good dark pencil line for your eye to follow as you cut. Remember that both of these saws have deadly sharp teeth, so plan the cut carefully.

2 Using the diagram as a guide, mark the side pieces with the angle that will form the roof slope of the bin.

3 Cut the front of the box to full size and then cut off the flap at the bottom.

4 On the panels, mark out, drill and countersink the holes to attach the batten frame. There are a lot of pilot holes to drill, and at the next stage a lot of screws to drive, and a Stanley ratchet screwdriver or a Bosch battery screwdriver/drill will speed the job along.

5 Glue and screw all the framing battens to the two side panels. The top edges of the two vertical battens, and both ends of the top horizontal ones, need to be cut at an angle to match the panels. Notice the fancy little joint I created at the front – but don't worry, if you can't cut this joint, because it won't make any difference to the strength of the bin.

6 Before attaching the front and back, glue and screw a short batten of timber on the inside of each side panel in the position where the handles will go outside. Plywood is strong, but the handle screws need something more substantial to bite into, otherwise the handles will simply come away in your hands when you try to lift the box.

7 Glue and screw the back and front in place. Check for squareness at this stage. If the bin is not square, lean heavily on one corner and check again – it will surprise you how easily it can be squared up before the glue dries.

8 Turn the bin over; assemble the five tongue-and-groove boards that form the base, removing the tongue from one outer edge and the groove from the other for neatness. Glue and screw the boards on to the batten frame at the bottom of the bin, then fix the feet to the base.

9 Before turning the bin back over, bore drainage holes in the base. Use a flat bit, developed especially for this sort of job.

10 Now assemble the pieces for the flap at the front. Glue and screw the hinge support beam to the outside of the fixed front panel. Screw the hinges to the top of the flap and the two bolts to the bottom before screwing the hinges to the front panel, aligning them with the support beam. Do not make it a tight fit as it will expand, and possibly jam, in the constantly damp conditions it has to endure. Screw the bolt keeper plates to blocks of wood, which are then attached under the floor. In reality you will find that the compost does not exert a lot of pressure on these bolts.

ROOF

1 Assemble the shiplap boards that make the roof, making a small curve on each end of the corner pieces (see diagram on page 69) using a jigsaw. Prepare the two battens that run underneath, not forgetting to shape their ends, too.

2 Measure accurately where the screw holes in the shiplap boards go: when fitted, the battens should be flush with the outside of the store's side panels. I pencil in the screw holes on one board, offer it up to the store to ensure that it fits, and then mark all the other screw holes from this one piece. Do not make it a tight fit as it will get damp and you don't want it to jam on top of the bin. Drill and countersink the holes in the shiplap. Now, glue and screw the shiplap boards to the battens. As the job progresses, keep checking that the battens do not move. Remember that glue is slippery until it dries, and if you make an error here, it is possible that the roof will not fit.

3 At the top edge of the bin back, fix one back support batten. Fix the other one to the roof by attaching it to the side support battens: this prevents the roof slipping off.

FINISH

Use a wood-care product as described on page 19. Particular attention must be paid to the inside, which will be damper than the outside, and for this I recommend Ronseal 5-Year Woodstain. Be generous and give the bin two coats. If you've made the shredder store as well, choose colours that will match.

CORNER SEAT
AND TRELLIS

Most gardens have a secluded corner or a hidden-away shady place that are havens of peace. This seat will enable you to enjoy a quiet sit down and, even if a surprise shower passes overhead, you will also be able to keep dry. I have turned the roof uprights into trellis, onto which a variety of climbing plants can be trained.

Unlike some garden seats, this is a really comfortable one to sit on. Imagine a large cushion at your back – are you comfortably seated? – enjoy the garden, admire the view and forget the weeds!

It is a strong structure, too. Mine fits on the corner of my decking, so I took the precaution of bolting the feet to the deck. It has experienced tremendous gusts of wind and rain, but remains upright with the roof on.

Dimensions

Height   77in (1956mm)
Width   (top) 68in (1727mm)
Depth   36in (914mm)

Tools

Pencil, expanding rule, Jetcut saw, smoothing plane, Bosch jigsaw, Bosch battery drill/screwdriver, drill bits, countersink, Bosch router.

Sundries

Several hundred galvanized screws (No. 8s: 1¼in/32mm, 1½in/38mm and 2½in/63mm), glue, coach bolts, wood-care product.

Timber

All the timber sizes are stock standard, so you should have no difficulties. The battens for the trellis are best as sawn timber, which gives climbing plants a much rougher texture to grip as they climb heavenwards. The roof is made from shiplap boarding, which avoids roofing felt, bitumen and galvanized felt nails.

Cutting List

Feet	2	38 x 3 x 1½in (965 x 76 x 38mm)
Roof supports	2	40 x 3 x 1½in (1016 x 76 x 38mm)
Main uprights (front)	2	74½ x 3 x 1½in (1892 x 76 x 38mm)
Main uprights (back)	2	69½ x 3 x 1½in (1765 x 76 x 38mm)
Trellis horizontals	20	27 x 2 x 1in (686 x 50 x 25mm)
Trellis verticals	6	64 x 2 x 1in (1626 x 50 x 25mm)
Front trellis batten	2	70 x 2 x 1in (1778 x 50 x 25mm)
SEAT		
Bearers	2	34 x 3 x 1½in (864 x 76 x 38mm)
Front support	1	46 x 5 x ⅞in (1168 x 127 x 22mm)
Slats	5	*cut to fit from 5 x ⅞in (127 x 22mm)*
ROOF		
Shiplap	12	64½ x 5½ x ¾in (1636 x 140 x 19mm)
		reducing in size down to 17½ x 5½ x ¾in (444 x 140 x 19mm)
Frame sides	2	58 x 3 x 1½in (1473 x 76 x 38mm)
Frame centre	1	33½ x 2 x 1in (851 x 50 x 25mm)
Frame front	1	68 x 3 x 1in (1727 x 76 x 25mm)
Frame back	1	14¼ x 3 x 1in (362 x 76 x 25mm)

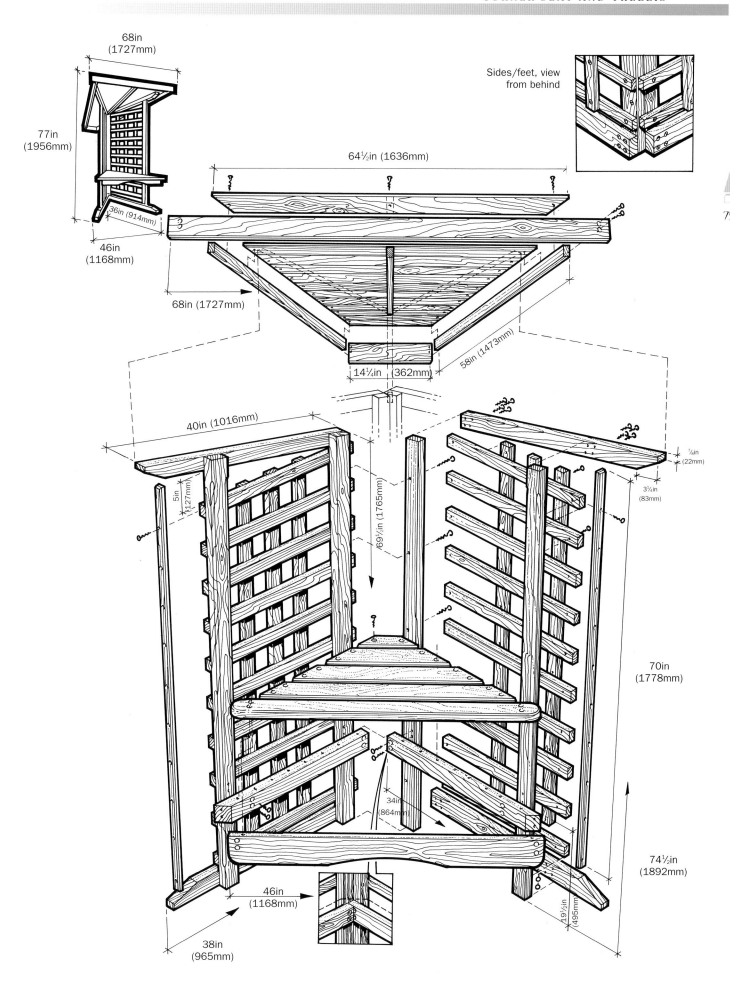

68in
(1727mm)

77in
(1956mm)

36in (914mm)

46in
(1168mm)

68in (1727mm)

64½in (1636mm)

Sides/feet, view
from behind

58in (1473mm)

14¼in   (362mm)

40in (1016mm)

⅞in
(22mm)

3¼in
(83mm)

5in
(127mm)

69½in (1765mm)

70in
(1778mm)

74½in
(1892mm)

34in
(864mm)

19½in
(495mm)

46in
(1168mm)

38in
(965mm)

Design Tip

This item is basically two identical sides with a seat slung between and a roof on top, so it makes sense to make the two sides at the same time; cutting the timber for both together will save you a great deal of time. However, when it comes to construction, do not forget there is a left- and a right-hand side.

Construction

1 Cut to length the feet, sawing and then planing the shapes on the ends. Do exactly the same for the roof timbers at the top.

2 Now cut to length the four main uprights, both front and back.

3 Find a good flat workspace (garage floor) and assemble the feet, the main uprights and the roof timbers. Glue and screw the units together, and then check to see that they are square. You will need to use four screws at each junction – gauge 10 is ideal. Do not forget to glue the joints because this will add tremendous rigidity to the structure.

4 Place the two side frames flat on the floor, inside faces down. Cut the trellis horizontals to length and screw them on to the frames. Stanley Bostitch air tools enable you to do this part of the job at lightning speed: do not forget those eye protectors. Add a spot of glue beneath each joint to increase the strength of the whole structure.

5 At this point the two sides are lifted and joined at the back, so you will need the help of an assistant. First, however, drill pilot holes on one side, following the diagram. Have your assistant hold everything in place while you glue and screw the sides together, using the 2½in (63mm) screws. Check that they are at 90 degrees to each other, and if they are not, apply a little muscle power to one side in order to square up the structure.

SEAT

1 Now cut the seat bearers. These are glued and screwed on to the inside edges of the frame. As this is a seat for dreaming on, it is worth making sure it is the right height for you. To get the correct height, measure the distance from the bottom of your heel to the inside of your knee – in other words, the inside measurement for your lower leg. If you like your feet on the ground while sitting, this measurement will be right for you. If you are making the seat for your wife and you ask her for this vital measurement, she simply will not believe you – you have been warned...

2 Once the seat-bearer timbers have been fixed to the framework, you should trim off their front ends at 45 degrees. This needs to be done accurately with a Jetcut saw.

3 Using a jigsaw, cut the front seat support to shape. You will also need to round off all the sharp edges. If you have a router, this is a good time to use it fitted with a ball-bearing cutter (*see* page 12). Routers are very quick so always make certain that you have clamped the timber firmly down, that your safety specs are on and that the cable is out of harm's way. Like the bench (page 60–65), this is a good first routing project that will give you confidence to use the machine on more complicated jobs.

4 Cut the seat slats to fit. You can also use the router to shape their edges. Glue and screw them in place, starting from the back.

SIDES AND ROOF

1 The vertical slats of the trellis are now fitted on the outside edges. It is not necessary to put screws in at every junction (where the horizontal battens cross) – every other one should be sufficient.

2 A batten is screwed into the ends of all the horizontal battens. This is not a structural necessity, but it does make the job look neater. You can rout a decorative edge onto this batten if you wish, to add to the overall appearance.

3 The roof is made from shiplap boards with a simple framework of battens holding it together. Cut to length all the shiplap boards, allowing for the angles which can be cut in one go when the roof is fixed to the batten frame. This is the sure way of lining everything up.

4 The construction of the roof requires an assistant. Cut the battens to size and then assemble them on a flat surface, gluing and screwing them together. Place the shiplap boards on top. Be prepared for a lot of shuffling of boards until all is settled. On the shiplap, make pencil marks showing where the battens are underneath, to help you screw the shiplap boards to the battens. The assistant should be able to help to keep things steady. This is a bit fiddly, but patience pays off.

5 Once all the shiplap boards are screwed to the battens beneath, use a Jetcut saw to take off all the offcuts and make a perfectly formed roof.

FINISHING

Use a wood-care product as described on page 19. Here I have used Ronseal Garden Woodstain.

Carry the seat unit to where you are going to place it in the garden, and then fit the roof on to the seat using coach screws. This makes are very strong structure, and the roof will not get blown off in the wind. You must bore pilot holes for the coach screws, otherwise they will split the wood as you drive them in.

THE BRIDGE

This bridge is not in the class of the one painted by Monet in Giverny, but it will, I have no doubt, be a distinctive feature in any garden. Bridges are intended for crossing a chasm or stream, and as most gardens do not have these, a little ingenuity is called for. Perhaps the bridge could have shrubs or conifers behind it and a pebble pool in front. If this is done imaginatively, with a sprinkler effect from the pool, then it will be very effective, and crossing to the other side to view the water will be an interesting prospect.

The arrangement can be enhanced at night through the use of exterior lights. Try hiding them beneath the bridge so that light arcs upwards, or set a couple to shine on to the pool.

Dimensions

Height	49in (1245mm)
Width	85in (2159mm)
Depth	20in (508mm)

Tools

Pencil, expanding rule, Jetcut saw, hacksaw, spirit level, Bosch battery drill/screwdriver, drill bits, countersink, smoothing plane, Bosch jigsaw with a 'Progressor' blade, Bosch Belt sander, adjustable spanner.

Sundries

Zinc-plated screws (1½in/38mm, No. 8 and 2in/50mm, No. 10), zinc-plated coach bolts or studding rod. (Studding rod is a length of steel bar with continuous threading.

This has the added advantage that it can be cut to the correct length with a hacksaw, allowing for nuts and washers to go on the end); glue, wood-care product.

Timber

Ideally spruce, as it withstands outdoor conditions well. The bridge slats are made from roofing battens – be careful to select only those that are knot free, otherwise they might break when walked over.

Cutting List

BRIDGE

Feet	4	25 x 7 x 1in (645 x 178 x 25mm)
False feet	4	12 x 2 x 1in (305 x 50 x 25mm)
Steps	2	20 x 7 x 1in (508 x 178 x 25mm)
Step bearers	4	6½ x 1 x 1in (165 x 25 x 25mm)
Span	2	73¼ x 7 x 1in (1861 x 178 x 25mm)
Walkway battens	22	25½ x 2 x 1in (648 x 50 x 25mm)

HANDRAIL

End verticals	2	39 x 2 x 2in (991 x 50 x 50mm)
Centre verticals	2	29 x 2 x 1in (737 x 50 x 50mm)
Top rail	1	85 x 3 x 1in (2159 x 76 x 25mm)
Middle rail	2	31 x 2 x 1in (790 x 50 x 25mm)
Bottom rail	1	68 x 3 x 1in (1727 x 76 x 25mm)
Decorative square	1	9 x 9 x 1in (229 x 229 x 25mm)

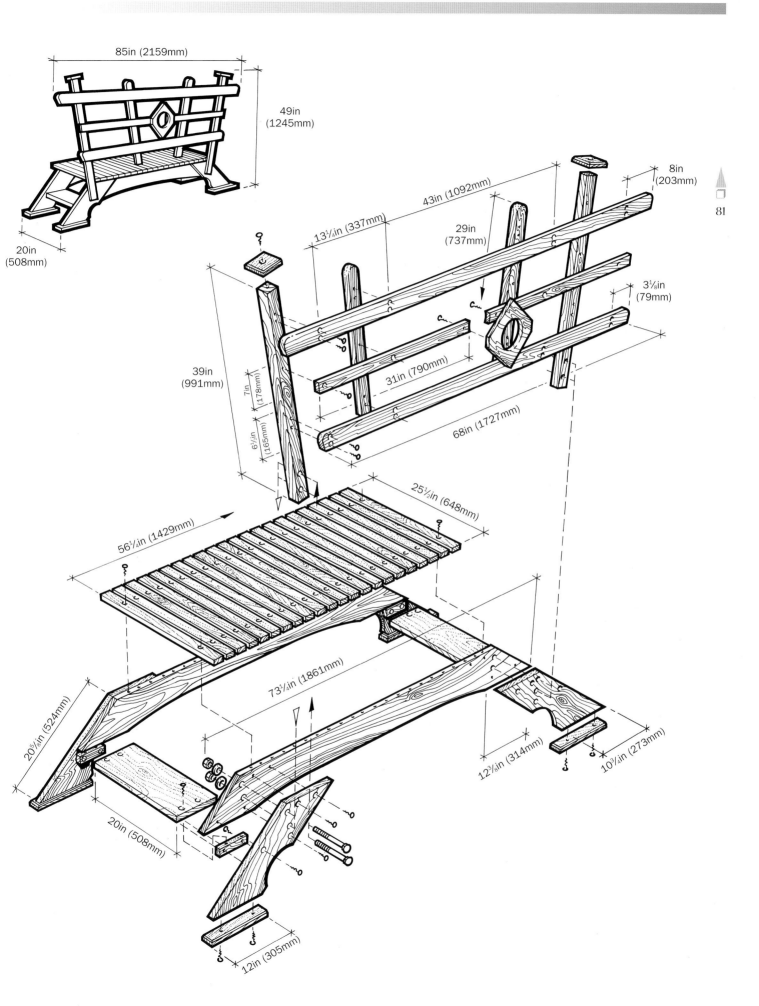

85in (2159mm)

49in
(1245mm)

20in
(508mm)

8in
(203mm)

43in (1092mm)

13¼in (337mm)

29in
(737mm)

3⅛in
(79mm)

39in
(991mm)

7in
(178mm)

6½in
(165mm)

31in (790mm)

68in (1727mm)

25½in (648mm)

56¼in (1429mm)

73¼in (1861mm)

20⅝in (524mm)

12¾in (314mm)

10¾in (273mm)

20in
(508mm)

12in (305mm)

Construction

1 Start with the bridge feet. They lift the bridge walkway over the 'stream', so you can, if you wish, increase their length and add an extra step to make the bridge higher. It is a good idea to make a cardboard template to get the curved shaping right. Don't forget that the ends are angled, so allow for this before marking and cutting the sections away. Use a 'Progressor' blade in the jigsaw to do the cutting of the curves, and a Jetcut saw to do the ends.

In all these cutting operations you must clamp the timber down firmly . It is one of the most obvious facts, but steel saw teeth cut fast and efficiently in wood and will absolutely massacre your fingers, if given half a chance – so always clamp up.

2 Inevitably, the timber that is in contact with the ground will deteriorate, so it is a good idea to make and screw on to the long feet some small false feet. These can be easily replaced when necessary and will prevent damage to the main feet timbers.

3 Cut to length the bridge steps, and the small lengths of timber that go underneath them to act as bearers. Glue and screw these to the inside edges of the feet.

4 You can now make a start on the span timbers. You could make a template of the curve, as for the feet, or use a line and pencil to mark it in, or you could use a thin flexible batten, hand held and bent to shape, while an assistant draws in the line to be cut. The deeper the curve, the less strength in the bridge walkway – so don't overdo it. Once again, the jigsaw and a Progressor blade is invaluable. If you do not use a Progressor blade, then you will have to use a spokeshave or a belt sander to remove all the saw-tooth marks.

5 Once the span timbers are shaped, they have to be glued and screwed to the feet. Choose a screw that has a good thick shank – a gauge 10 – and a length that will almost go right through. Pencil in the position of the screws on the feet – it is best to put them near the corners or edges. Drill and countersink the screw holes in the feet. Don't join the pieces together yet.

6 Using a Stanley knife, key the insides of the timbers to be joined. The knife cuts allow the glue to get right into the fibres of the timber, thus increasing the gluing area and adding to the strength of the joint. Use generous amounts of glue, and wipe the faces of the timbers against one another to make sure it is well spread in the joint.

Now align the foot with the span and screw the pieces together. It helps if the pieces are clamped together at this stage. The glue will tend to make the timber slip, so as you tighten the screws, keep checking that the pieces are still aligned. One of the great advantages of a battery screwdriver is the rapid driving in of screws. If the alignment is not perfect, it is easy to put the screwdriver into reverse, extract the screw, and start again.

Repeat the operation for all the other feet.

7 Now the two steps can be glued and screwed in place on to the bearers. At this stage, it helps to place the bridge on a flat area while the assembly goes on. It is important to check that once the steps are glued in place, the sides are at 90 degrees to the ground – you don't want a lop-sided bridge.

8 Now cut the battens for the bridge walkway. If you buy roofing battens in a bundle, now is the time to sort them out. Reject all those lengths that have big knots. This will probably involve quite a bit of cutting. Do not worry about the waste – batten makes perfect lighting wood for the fire!

9 Glue and screw the battens in place along the top of the bridge spans. Do be careful to keep them all aligned – nothing looks worse than a straggly line of battens at either side. Drive a screw into each end of the spans and attach a length of cord between them. You can use this to line up each batten as you go.

HANDRAIL

1 Cut the vertical handrails to length and, following the diagram, bore the holes to take coach bolts or threaded studding rod. You will need to use a mains-powered drill for these holes; be careful that you position them well away from the screws that hold the feet. Attach the vertical posts to the bridge with bolts or threaded studding rod; don't forget the washers beneath the nut heads.

2 Now cut the top and bottom horizontal rails to length, shape their ends with a jigsaw and screw them to the vertical posts.

3 Cut and shape the two short centre verticals. These must be screwed in place before the middle horizontal rail can be fixed. This rail is in two parts joined by a decorative wooden block with a circular cut-out (see step 4 below).

4 Cut a suitable piece of wood into a square. Use a compass to mark the circle in the centre. To cut this out, you will need to clamp the piece of wood and use your jigsaw. First, in the area to be removed, drill three or four holes in a line – a chain of holes – and enlarge them until they run into each other. With the wood still firmly clamped down, insert the jigsaw blade into the holes and cut the circle. Do not force the jigsaw sideways, but rather steer it into the cut. Saw off two of the corners, for added decoration. If you use a 'Progressor' blade, you will not need to use glasspaper to smooth anything off. The decorative piece is now glued and screwed to the central horizontal rail.

5 End grain is particularly vulnerable to attack by water and algae. To guard against this and save yourself repair work later on, protect the main vertical posts by making up two little wooden cups to screw on to the ends.

FINISHING

Use a wood-care product as described on page 19. Here, I have used three colours of Ronseal Woodstain: Harvest Gold for the walkway slats, Evergreen for the spans and Terracotta for the handrails.

OLD VILLAGE PUMP

Springs, wells and pumps have traditionally always been a meeting place where people congregate. I have tried to capture in this project something of a world gone by in this charming water pump. The sound of running water is very restful and soothing, so I decided that I would install a small electrically powered pump to recycle water inside the trough. To add further interest, I asked a friend to make a small bucket and a copper spout. Like this I get the trickle of water into the first bucket and then from the bucket into the trough – two lots of splashes for the price of one. If your woodwork is not quite up to being water tight, this project looks equally good as an eye-catching planter!

Dimensions

Height	36in (914mm)
Width	30in (762mm)
Depth	19in (483mm)

Warning

If you decide to fit the pump yourself, be sure to get an electrician to check your work before you turn everything on.

Do take professional advice – the combination of water and electricity are killers, and you will not get a second chance.

Cutting List

TROUGH

Base T&G board	3	24 x 3¾ x ¾in (610 x 95 x 19mm)
Legs	2	16⅝ x 2¾ x 1in (422 x 70 x 25mm)
Feet	4	4¾ x 2¾ x 1in (121 x 70 x 25mm)
End pieces (lowest)	2	16⅛ x 3¾ x ¾in (410 x 95 x 19mm)
End pieces (centre)	2	17 x 3¾ x ¾in (432 x 95 x 19mm)
End pieces (top)	2	17 x 3¾ x ¾in (432 x 95 x 19mm)
Side pieces	6	24 x 3¾ x ¾in (610 x 95 x 19mm)

PUMP

Top	1	7¼ x 6 x ⅞in (184 x 152 x 22mm)
Sides	2	27 x 3⅝ x ¾in (686 x 92 x 19mm)
Front (below spout)	1	20 x 3¼ x ¾in (508 x 83 x 19mm)
Front (above spout)	1	3½ x ¾ x ¾in (89 x 19 x 19mm)
Back (slotted)	1	27 x 3¾ x ¾in (686 x 95 x 19mm)
Handle	1	20 x 4 x ⅞in (508 x 102 x 22mm)
Spout sides	2	7 x 3 x ½in (178 x 76 x 13mm)
Spout base	1	7¾ x 1 x ½in (197 x 76 x 13mm)

TROUGH TOP

Sides	2	27½ x 2¾ x 1in (698 x 70 x 25mm)
Ends	2	13½ x 2¾ x 1in (348 x 70 x 25mm)
Slips of wood	2	cut to fit
Mouldings	3	cut to fit

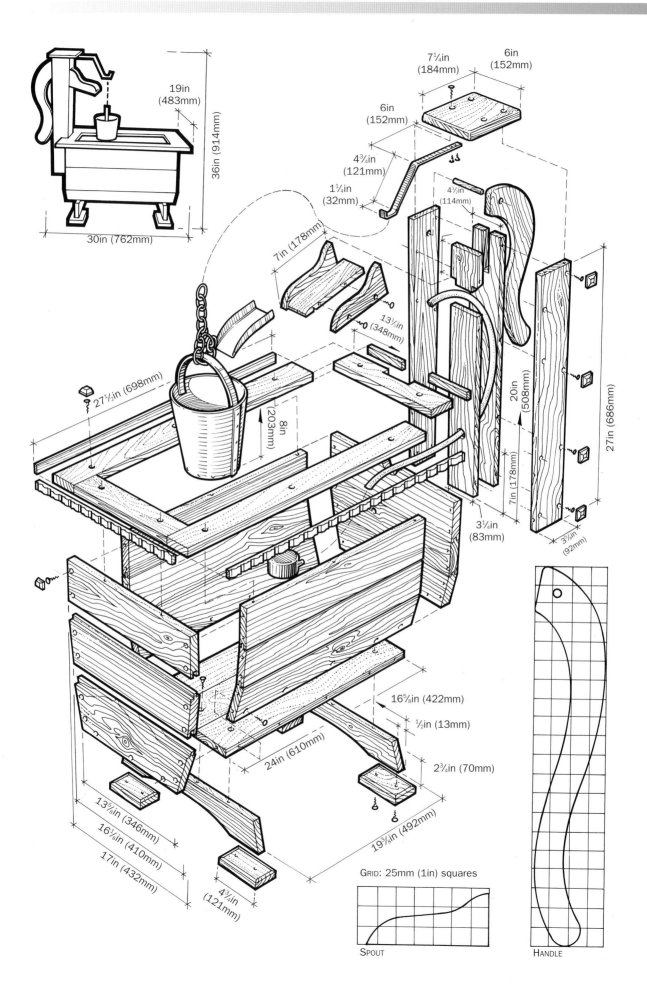

19in
(483mm)

36in (914mm)

30in (762mm)

7¼in
(184mm)

6in
(152mm)

6in
(152mm)

4¾in
(121mm)

1¼in
(32mm)

4½in
(114mm)

7in (178mm)

13½in
(348mm)

27½in (698mm)

8in
(203mm)

20in
(508mm)

27in (686mm)

7in (178mm)

3¼in
(83mm)

3⅝in
(92mm)

16⅝in (422mm)

½in (13mm)

2¾in (70mm)

24in (610mm)

19⅜in (492mm)

13⅝in (346mm)

16⅛in (410mm)

17in (432mm)

4¾in
(121mm)

Grid: 25mm (1in) squares

Spout

Handle

Tools

Pencil, expanding rule, carpenter's square, Jetcut saw, Bosch battery screwdriver/drill, drill bits, countersink, smoothing plane, chisels, Bosch jigsaw, Bosch orbital sander.

Sundries

Water pump (Hozelock make a selection), length of rubber hose (the type used in car radiator systems), dowel rod, cast-iron studs (for an aged look), metal hook, small metal bucket, chain, shaped metal mouthpiece, waterproof glue (Cascamite One Shot is ideal for this project), and a wood-care product.

Timber

To get the barrel shape, you will need to buy tongue-and-groove board. There is a variety that has one of its sides planed off, leaving a nice decorative groove, and it is this groove that helps to make the boards sufficiently flexible to produce a curved barrel shape for the trough sides. The base is ordinary tongue-and-groove spruce. The pump body is from Nordic red pine, and the mouldings around the edge are from the widely available Richard Burbidge collection.

Design Tip

The metal mouthpiece directs the water more accurately than a wooden one. Look in your local telephone directory for an engineering firm that can fabricate the metal parts for you – it shouldn't be very expensive.

Construction
TROUGH

1 Cut to length the tongue-and-groove boards for the base. Now cut out the legs. Mark out the curve (see page 36, steps 3 and 4) on the underside of the legs and use a jigsaw to cut it out. Each leg end slopes slightly; cut the angle with a Jetcut saw.

2 Now cut the four small feet; shape them using a hand plane before screwing them on to the legs. Drill and countersink the holes first.

3 To assemble the base, mix the waterproof glue and run it into the grooves in the boards. Rub the boards together making sure that the glue is worked well in to the grooves – not only will this glue the boards together, it will also waterproof the joints. Once the glue is cured, screw the legs to the base. The screws are driven from the top down into the legs.

4 Now begins the task of building up the sides, a layer at a time. do steps 4 to 6 as a dry run first, before gluing and screwing everything in place.

Cut to length the pieces that make up the two ends of the trough. Now experiment with two tongue-and-groove boards, straining them to see just how much of an angle you can make with them. It is this angle that determines the angle you have to cut on the end pieces. It sounds more difficult than it is. Cut this angle at either end of the lowest end pieces before gluing and screwing them in place.

5 Cut to length the side tongue-and-groove boards. Select the board that will be at the base of one side, and mark on the bottom edge the angle that will need to be planed off to make a tidy job. Repeat for the other side. The two sides are then glued and screwed to the base and the ends. Be careful to align the tongue-and-groove sections.

6 Now fit the next side pieces on to the tongues of the boards below, and 'strain' them inwards – it is this angle that helps the barrel shape to form. Mark this angle on to the centre end pieces so that you can cut it out. Repeat the process for the top layer of boards.

7 When you are ready to screw and glue the sides and ends together, you will need to run the glue into the grooves of the boards to waterproof the joints.

PUMP

1 Cut and shape all the sections of the pump body. Use the template to size up and mark up the shapes for the handle and the spout, and use a jigsaw to cut them out. The handle is purely decorative, but it is fun!

2 Before gluing and screwing the various pieces together, following the diagram carefully, insert the length of tubing into the pump body, through a drilled hole that is slightly larger than the tubing. Don't forget to fit the metal spout into the wooden one. The pump handle is held in place with a length of dowel rod. And before you add the top, insert the metal hook to hold the bucket.

TROUGH TOP

1 The surrounds for the top of the trough are next. I simply butt-jointed these at the corners, but if you wish, you can cut mitres. Glue and screw them to the top of the trough.

2 Before fitting the end nearest the pump, screw the pump body to the trough. Only when this is done can you cut the shape for the trough surround for that end. The small area of wood to be removed can easily be cut away with a jigsaw.

FINISHING

In my builder's merchant I found some forged studs that simply screw into the timber. You can place these randomly, using their heads to cover up any screws that are too obvious. Alternatively, wait until the glue has dried, and extract the ordinary screws and put the forged studs in their place.

Mouldings around the edge of the trough just set it off. You may think that it is a bit fancy, but the old village pump on which I modelled this one has little stone carvings all around the trough, and these look good.

Before fitting the pump and turning on the water, coat the trough and pump body with a wood-care product as described on page 19. I was very generous with my choice of wood preservative – Ronseal 5-Year Woodstain – and suggest you apply two coats to make sure the water does not get to the wood.

I turned my pump on and yes, it worked, although the water did not go exactly where I had planned. I had some adjustments to make with the feed pipe and the spout. But all the effort was eventually worth it, because it makes a really lovely garden, patio, conservatory or even porch door entrance feature.

SHREDDER STORE

I suppose it happens in all households: you build a new shed and it looks big and roomy – that is until you start to put things into it. It is only a matter of weeks before it fills up with bicycles, seed potatoes, the odd tent – you name it, it's in there. And then, the ultimate frustration, you go to get something and it is right at the very back!

I have always wanted a shredder, but the thought of another implement inaccessible through the clutter was unbearable. Then I came up with the idea for a purpose-built shed for the shredder – just big enough for a shredder, and nothing, absolutely nothing else.

Dimensions

Height	49¾in (1264mm)
Width	29⅞in (759mm)
Depth	25in (635mm)

Tools

Pencil, expanding rule, protractor, carpenter's square, Bosch battery drill/screwdriver, drill bits, countersink, Bosch circular saw, Jetcut saw, smoothing plane.

Sundries

Two T-strap hinges: 9in (229mm), two bolts, a pair of handles, zinc-plated screws (1½in/38mm, No. 8 and 2in/50mm, No. 8), black japanned round-headed screws (¾in/19mm, No. 8) for the hinges, glue, wood-care product.

Cutting List

Back and side panels (plywood)	3	48¾ x 25 x ½in (1238 x 635 x 13mm)
Floor (T&G board)	5	25 x 5½ x ⅞in (635 x 140 x 22mm)
Feet	2	25 x 2 x 2in (635 x 50 x 50mm)
STORE FRAME		
Back battens	2	48¾ x 2 x 1in (1238 x 50 x 25mm)
Front battens	2	42 x 2 x 1in (1067 x 50 x 25mm)
Top battens	2	24⅝ x 2 x 1in (626 x 50 x 25mm)
Bottom battens (side)	2	23 x 2 x 1in (584 x 50 x 25mm)
Bottom battens (back)	1	25 x 2 x 1in (635 x 50 x 25mm)
Front (shaped) batten	1	21 x 2 x 2in (533 x 50 x 50mm)
DOOR		
Door (plywood)	1	40 x 21 x ½in (1016 x 533 x 13mm)
Side battens	2	40 x 2 x 1in (1016 x 50 x 25mm)
Cross battens	4	19 x 2 x 1in (483 x 50 x 25mm)
Hinge supports	2	17 x 2 x 1in (432 x 50 x 25mm)
Plinth	1	20¾ x 3 x 1in (527 x 76 x 25mm)
Roof shiplap	7	29⅞ x 4½ x ⅝in (759 x 114 x 16mm)
Roof support battens	2	30⅜ x 2¾ x 1in (772 x 70 x 25mm)
Handle strengthener	2	11 x 3 x 1in (279 x 76 x 25mm)

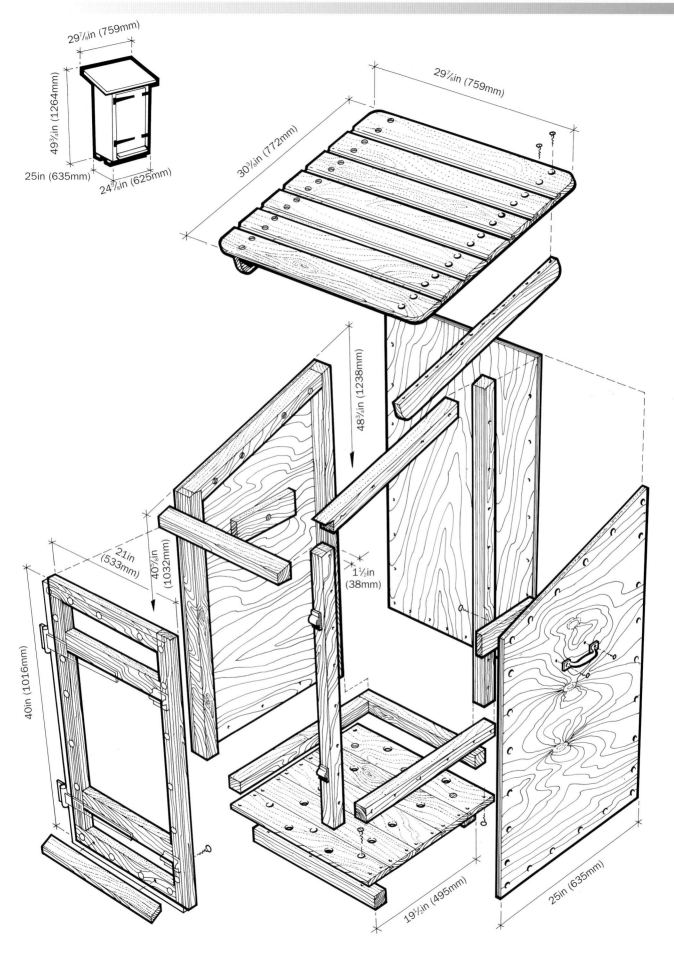

29⅞in (759mm)

49¾in (1264mm)

25in (635mm)

24⅜in (625mm)

29⅞in (759mm)

30⅜in (772mm)

48¾in (1238mm)

21in (533mm)

40⅝in (1032mm)

1½in (38mm)

40in (1016mm)

19½in (495mm)

25in (635mm)

Timber

I do not like waste, so I designed the shed so that all four sides would cut from a standard sheet of 8 x 4ft (2.5 x 1.2m) water- and boil-proof plywood (WBP). Besides the plywood, spruce is a good choice. You do not need to buy the planed variety but sawn timbers will do perfectly for the frame. Tongue-and-groove floor boarding is also necessary, and a good quality shiplap board for the roof.

Construction
STORE

1 Mark out the side panels on the sheet of plywood. See the Compost Bin (pages 66–71) for details on how to ensure a safe and easy cut, using either a mains-powered circular saw or a Jetcut one.

2 Using the diagram for measurements, shape the two side panels to produce the slope necessary for the roof.

3 Cut the door to size.

4 Now make the floor. Cut the tongue-and-groove boards to length and slot them together. On one outer edge remove the tongue, and on the other outer edge, the groove. Cut and fit the two full-length battens to go under the floor. These will keep the store off the ground. Bore a few holes in the floor to allow air to circulate.

5 Drill screw pilot holes in the side panels to secure the batten frame. Now glue and screw all the battens to the inside edges of the panels. The top edges of the two vertical battens, and both ends of the top horizontal ones, need to be cut at an angle at their ends to match the panels.

Notice the fancy little joint I created at the front – don't worry if you can't cut this joint, as it won't make any difference to the strength of the store.

6 Once the battens are all screwed to the sides, the back can be attached. Make sure that the edges are square to the sides.

7 The front batten to hold the sides together is now shaped to fit. Pencil in the angle and the section of wood to be planed off. A sharp smoothing plane is the perfect tool for shaping this piece. I emphasize sharp – if your's has been used to prop the shed door open for the last two years, buy yourself a new one. A sharp plane is a joy to use – it whistles as it cuts.

8 Glue and screw the shaped piece in place between the two front frame battens. Use the 2in/50mm screws. This also forms the top of the doorway.

9 Turn the box upside down and screw the floor to the frame battens that run along the back and the sides.

10 Glue and screw blocks of timber inside the store to act as anchorage points for the handles. The plywood sides are

strong, but the screws holding the handles must have something substantial to bite into, otherwise the first time you use the handles, they will come off in your hands.

DOOR

1 The door comes next and this, like the plywood sides, has a framework glued and screwed on to the inside edges. Note the two extra horizontal bracing bars; these provide anchorage for the screws that hold the hinges to the door.

2 To prevent water getting into the box, a plinth is now fitted to the bottom of the door. This has a slight angle on it to shed the water. Carefully mark in pencil the wood that has to be removed, and use a smoothing plane to remove it.

3 The plinth is attached to the door with glue and two large screws that are of sufficient length to sink well into the plinth and hold it to the door front. Care is necessary to ensure that these do not 'break out' onto the nicely planed front edge of the plinth as they are fitted. Pre-bore two large holes through the bottom of the door frame inside, push through the screws that you intend to use, and the length that they protrude will show where

they will come to in the plinth. You can measure the length of the screw, but this is a 'dead reckoning' method.

4 Now try fitting the door into the frame. Don't be tempted to make this a very tight fit, because when you move the store to its final position, the frame will move and the door might stick. T-strap hinges are used on all shed doors. These screw straight on to the door and the frame. Be certain to position them to line up with the cross battens of the frame. Now fix in place the bolts that will hold the door shut.

5 Once the door is in place, you will discover that as it opens, the plinth fouls the frame. Use a tenon saw to cut off a small portion on the hinge side, just enough to allow the door to open freely.

ROOF

1 Assemble the shiplap boards that make the roof, removing the sharp corners with a jigsaw. Prepare the two battens that run underneath, not forgetting to shape their ends, too.

2 Measure accurately where the screw holes in the shiplap boards go when fitted, the

battens should be flush with the outside of the store's side panels. I pencil in the screw holes on one board, offer it up to the store to ensure that it fits, and then mark all the other screw holes from this one piece. Now you can drill and countersink the holes in the shiplap, and glue and screw the shiplap boards to the battens. As the job progresses, keep checking that the battens do not move. Glue is slippery until it dries, and if you make an error here, it is possible that the roof will not fit.

3 Place the roof in position and screw it to the store through the side battens.

FINISHING

Use a wood-care product as described on page 19. Here I have used Ronseal Garden Woodstain, blue for the base and yellow (Pine) for the roof.

KIDS' PLAYHOUSE

Because children have such active imaginations, a den is really an essential part of growing up – it allows a young mind to take wings. This great playhouse can become anything from a space station to a wilderness log cabin. It can be a ship on the Spanish Main. Or you can make it your very own observation hut, deep in the thickest jungle – where *you* can hide from the children.

The end can be panelled with tongue-and-groove floorboarding, which makes a very nice finish, or for speed use a sheet of plywood. Whichever you decide, you will be very surprised at how much of a den you get for your money, because the timber frames make a good-sized playhouse.

Dimensions

Height	55¾in (1416mm)
Depth	47½in (1207mm)
Width	53in (1346mm)

Tools

Pencil, expanding rule, carpenter's square, protractor, Jetcut panel and tenon saw, Bosch battery screwdriver/drill, drill bits, countersink, Bosch jigsaw, six or eight clamps, chisels, mallet, smoothing plane.

Sundries

Zinc-plated screws, perspex corrugated sheets, glue, wood-care product.

Timber

Use planed timber to avoid splinters. For the end wall, use tongue-and-groove boards or a sheet of WPB plywood.

Cutting List

END FRAMES

Bottom	2	45 x 3 x 1in (1143 x 76 x 25mm)
Sides	4	44½ x 3 x 1in (1130 x 76 x 25mm)
Roof apex (left)	2	37 x 3 x 1in (940 x 76 x 25mm)
Roof apex (right)	2	33¾ x 3 x 1in (857 x 76 x 25mm)
Plates	2	10 x 3 x 1in (254 x 76 x 25mm)
Window upper	1	55 x 3 x 1in (1397 x 76 x 25mm)
Window lower	1	45¾ x 3 x 1in (1162 x 76 x 25mm)
Panelling (above window) T&G board	11	16 x 5 x ⅝in (406 x 127 x 16mm)
Panelling (below window) T&G board	10	21 x 5 x ⅝in (533 x 127 x 16mm)
Door uprights	2	20½ x 2 x 1in (521 x 50 x 25mm)
Door horizontals	2	16½ x 2 x 1in (419 x 50 x 25mm)

SIDES AND ROOF

Main horizontals	8	47½ x 2 x 1in (1207 x 50 x 25mm)
Roof horizontals	6	47½ x 2 x 1in (1207 x 50 x 25mm)
Barge boards	4	37 x 5 x 1in (940 x 127 x 25mm)
Side verticals	4	17 x 2 x 1in (432 x 50 x 25mm)
Perspex	4	60½ x 30in (1537 x 762mm)

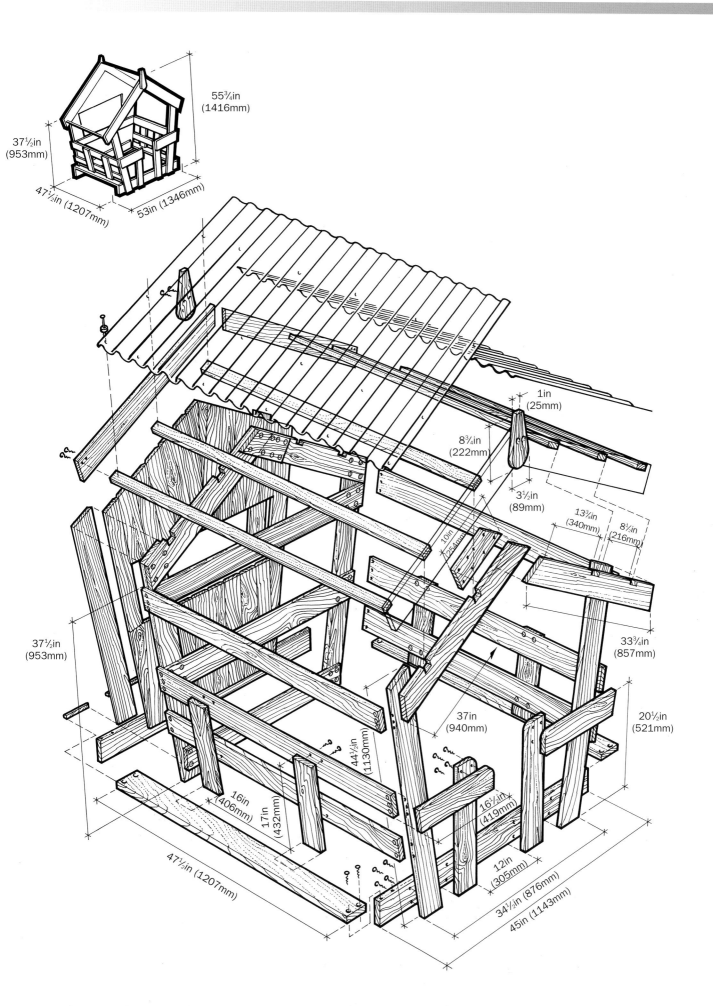

55¾in (1416mm)

37½in (953mm)

47½in (1207mm)

53in (1346mm)

1in (25mm)

8¾in (222mm)

3½in (89mm)

13⅜in (340mm)

8½in (216mm)

10in (254mm)

37½in (953mm)

33¾in (857mm)

20½in (521mm)

37in (940mm)

44½in (1130mm)

16in (406mm)

17in (432mm)

16½in (419mm)

47½in (1207mm)

12in (305mm)

34½in (876mm)

45in (1143mm)

Tip

Traditionally, the perspex corrugated sheeting is fitted as per the drawing, but you can fit it horizontally. This makes it more economical, but it will not shed water so efficiently, although it would keep a shower off. You will find that a slight overlapping of sheets is all that is required to keep the wet out.

You will need an assistant to help with assembly.

Construction
END FRAMES

1 Getting the end frames right is the most time-consuming part of the project. Begin with the door end. The most critical bit is marking out the angles at which the five main battens are glued and screwed together. Mark a centre line in the middle of the bottom timber. Mark the positions of the two sides. They should be 34½in (876mm) apart to their outside edges (see diagram). The two roof apex timbers are laid onto the two sides. Use a set square from the centre line on the bottom timber to give you their position at the top. All this sounds complicated, but work at it logically and it does come right. While all this setting out is going on you will need some clamps to hold the different bits together.

2 When you are happy with the end frame, pencil in exactly where the pieces of timber go, before releasing the clamps, cutting off the necessary angles and gluing and screwing everything together. Look at the diagram where the roof apex timbers meet – note the wood 'plate' screwed behind to hold them together. You cannot have one timber lying proud on the surface of the other, they must be

flush. A Jetcut tenon saw is ideal for the fine accurate cuts needed on these timbers.

3 Use the door end frame to mark out and build the window end frame. This saves time and aggravation.

4 When both end frames are finished, clamp them together to mark where the cut-outs for the roof timbers need to be. In this way the slots will line up between the frames – always a good idea!

Release the clamps and mark the depth of the slots. Either use a jigsaw to cut out the pieces or make a series of cuts with the tenon saw and then chisel out the pieces of wood. Use a mallet rather than a hammer to strike the chisel. Its large wooden head will not damage the chisel handle, and you are far less likely to miss the chisel and knock your own hand.

5 Now take the window end frame, and cut and screw in place the three horizontal inner timbers. Begin to fit the tongue-and-groove panelling from the middle of the bottom section, cutting and planing the boards as you go. On the upper section it is probably easier to work from the outside edges, which will leave you with a triangle shape to fill in the middle. There are many ways of doing this job – give it a bit of thought before you rush in.

6 Now turn your efforts to the door end frame. It really is a fairly quick and simple job to cut and fit these timbers, but DO make certain that you carefully round off the corners: it is always dangerous to leave corners and sharp edges where children play.

SIDES AND ROOF

1 The two frames are held together with eight main horizontal battens, and you will need an assistant to hold them while you get some of the battens in place. Do check that the frames are upright (90 degrees to the ground) before fixing. After the first few battens are in place, the structure becomes very rigid. The lowest main horizontals are screwed to the bottom end frame before the two short uprights are fitted.

2 Now cut and fit the battens that form the roof timbers. These will need to be fitted into the notches you cut into the end frames (End Frames, step 4). Glue and screw them in place.

3 To finish off the roof, fit the four barge boards onto the outside of the end frame main apex timbers, screwing them into the end grain of the roof battens as well. Be very careful to remove any sharp corners, as children running around the house may collide with the edges, and smooth rounded ends will cause far less hurt.

FINISH

This is one of those awkward situations, in that you cannot really apply wood preservative with the perspex in place – and do not kid yourself that you can paint around the timbers, because you can't. You will have to make a choice – for me, it is to treat all the timbers before you fit the perspex.

Use a wood-care product as described on page 19. Here, I have used Ronseal Quick-Drying Woodstain.

When it comes to fitting the perspex, use a very sharp fine-toothed Jetcut saw or a Bosch jigsaw fitted with a fine blade. The secret of cutting this material and boring holes in it, is not to force the saw or drill. Support the perspex beneath and at its edges, and let the cutting tool do the job in its own time. Always use a sharp saw or bit – blunt ones will cause radial cracks. I

have also found cutting more of a problem in cold weather. Don't bore holes in the valleys, only on the ridges. Water drains down the valleys, so screws fixed on the ridges are far less likely to let it in.

The perspex is fitted to the roof timbers with special screws and 'snap caps'. The latter totally enclose the screw heads, so when it rains, the water cannot seep down through the screw hole.

Safety is paramount when screwing the perspex to the roof, and it is very important that none projects over the sides or at the corners or edges; if it does you must trim it back.

Once everything is painted and the perspex is in place, cut, paint and fit the finials to finish off the roof ends.

MOWER STORE

Nowadays there is a huge range of garden aids: battery-powered hedge trimmers, strimmers, lawn vacuums, high-pressure jet washers – the list goes on. They all have one thing in common: they require storage space. I decided that I needed a purpose-built mower store, that also had room for other garden equipment. Now, when I want to cut the lawn, I want to get the mower out and be off, no fiddling with putting handles up and tightening bolts. With this in mind, I designed a long thin store, with a back wall and sides perfect for tidily storing everything else you might require. When you make your store, take a little time to fit hooks and shelves to take additional equipment – you will be forever grateful. Expanding luggage straps with a couple of hooks and eyes are very good for fixing big objects quickly.

Dimensions

Height	52½in (1333mm)
Width	70in (1778mm)
Depth	29in (737mm)

Tools

Pencil, expanding rule, builder's square, Stanley knife, Jetcut saw, spirit level, hammer, smoothing plane, Bosch battery drill/screwdriver, drill bits, countersink, Stanley Bostich air tool and compressor, Bosch electric planer.

Sundries

Nails, screws, four hinges, padlock hasp, medium density roofing felt, galvanized felt nails, glue.

Cutting List

Long floor bearers	2	66 x 2 x 2in (1676 x 50 x 50mm)
Short floor bearers	3	22 x 2 x 2in (559 x 50 x 50mm)
Feet	6	8 x 2 x 2in (203 x 50 x 50mm)
Floor boards (T&G)	13	26½ x 5½ x ⅞in (673 x 140 x 22mm)
Front corner posts	2	47 x 2 x 2in (1194 x 50 x 50mm)
Back corner posts	2	51½ x 2 x 2in (1308 x 50 x 50mm)
Back upright batten (centre)	1	42½ x 3 x 1in (1079 x 76 x 25mm)
Back upright battens (corners)	2	47½ x 3 x 1in (1206 x 76 x 25mm)
Back horizontal battens	2	70 x 3 x 1in (1778 x 76 x 25mm)
Side bracing posts	2	23½ x 2 x 2in (597 x 50 x 50mm)
Lintel	1	72¾ x 2 x 2in (1848 x 50 x 50mm)
Roofing battens (side)	2	24 x 2¾ x ⅞in (610 x 70 x 22mm)
Roofing battens (middle)	1	24 x 2 x 2in (610 x 50 x 50mm)
Roof (T&G)	6	80 x 5½ x ⅞in (2032 x 140 x 22mm)
Back wall (shiplap)	12	73½ x 4¾ x ¾in (1867 x 121 x 19mm)
Side wall (shiplap)	24	28⅛ x 4¾ x ¾in (714 x 121 x 19mm)
DOORS		
Frame verticals	4	42 x 3 x 2in (1067 x 76 x 50mm)
Frame horizontals	4	27½ x 3 x 2in (698 x 76 x 50mm)
Door fillers (shiplap)	20	33 x 4¾ x ¾in (838 x 121 x 19mm)

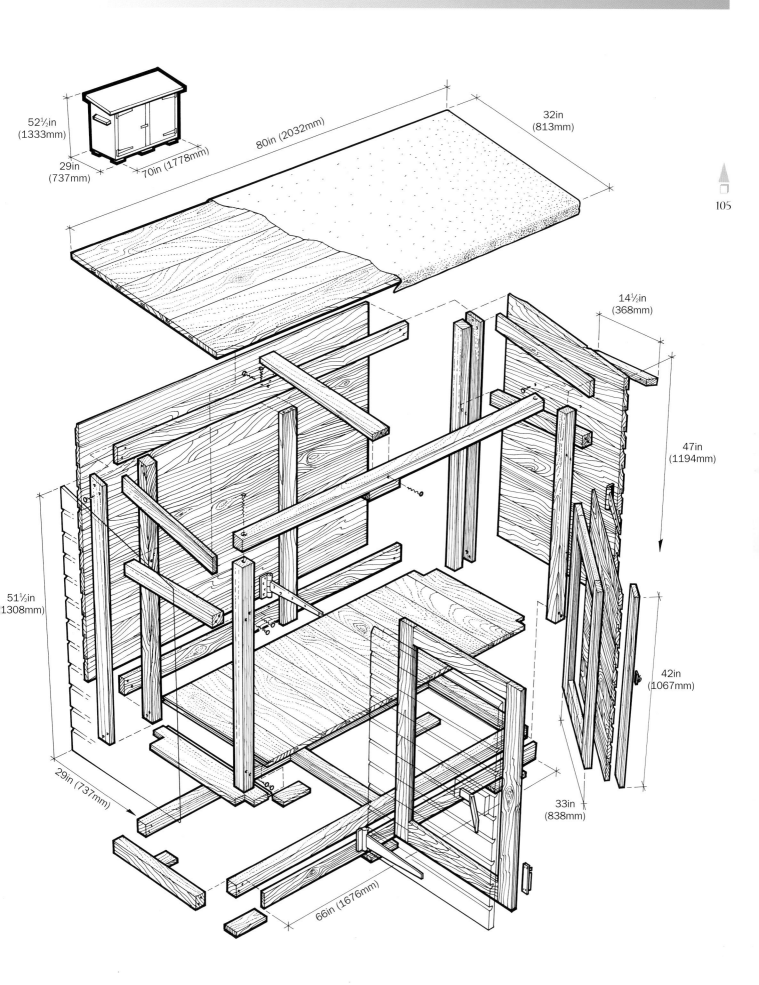

52½in
(1333mm)

29in
(737mm)

70in (1778mm)

80in (2032mm)

32in
(813mm)

14½in
(368mm)

47in
(1194mm)

51½in
(1308mm)

42in
(1067mm)

29in (737mm)

33in
(838mm)

66in (1676mm)

Timber

Make sure you have worked out the quantities of timber you need before you go shopping (remember to measure your mower and adjust this design to fit) and don't forget that most timber merchants have a home delivery service. If possible, use Nordic spruce: it is less expensive than red pine and is very happy outdoors. Tongue-and-groove floorboards and shiplap are both available in spruce.

Design Tip

I used a Stanley Bostich nailer to fix all the floorboards and all the shiplap to the sides and doors. Air-tools make the job much quicker, and the Stanley version, like all Stanley hand tools, is easy to use. Go to a hire shop and try one for a weekend – I am sure it will not be long before it is on your shopping list.

Technically this is not a difficult project, but it is heavy so as you get towards completion (fitting the roof), make sure that you have at least three helpers to assist when you position it in the garden.

Construction

1 Cut the floor bearers to length, making sure that you include a piece to go into the centre, as this is where the weight of the mower will be concentrated.

2 Glue and nail or screw the floor bearers together. Here the air-tool has a distinct advantage over a hammer: as you hammer in a nail, the whole structure shakes, but the air-tool shoots the nail in with the absolute minimum of vibration. If you choose screws, bore pilot holes first. Fit the six feet that go beneath the floor, one at each corner and one in the middle of each long side. These will keep the floor off the ground and protect it from rotting.

3 Cut all the tongue-and-groove floorboards to length, removing a tongue from one side and the corresponding groove from the other end. On these two end boards, you also have to cut out small squares in order to accommodate the four corner posts. It is advisable not to fix the floor until you have screwed the corner posts in place.

4 Cut the four corner posts to length. They are screwed to the corners of the floor. There are screws or nails already in this

area, so arrange the pilot holes to avoid these. Fix the back corner posts first. On to these, screw the two horizontal battens – one at the top, the other at the bottom. Now fix the two corner upright battens on to the corner posts. Finally, fix the centre upright batten, which goes flush between the two horizontal battens at the centre back of the store. The shiplap will be attached to these.

5 Now fix the front corner posts, taking care as you screw them into the floor (see step 4). Two screws in a diagonal line are best. Next, fit the bracing timbers between the front and back posts. These help to give stability to the front posts.

6 Attach the roofing battens that connect the tops of the back and front corner posts. This will give you the slope of the roof and thus the angle that the lintel must be shaped to. Pencil in the angle on the lintel before planing it off. A smoothing plane is a good tool for this, but an electric plane will do the job just as well. Whichever plane you decide to use, you must fix the timber firmly in the bench. Once the job is done, screw the lintel to the top of the front corner posts – this adds tremendous rigidity to the structure.

7 Now fix the middle roofing batten. This needs a couple of shallow angles cut in the ends before you can glue and screw it in place. If you do not take the trouble to cut these angles, using the lintel and back horizontal batten as templates, the roofing batten will not fit well and you will end up dissatisfied.

8 Nail the shiplap boards on to the frame at the sides and back. Cut the top side pieces at an angle along their length to fit the slope of the roof. Use oval nails to prevent the board from splitting. A Stanley Bostitch nailer gun will do the job in a quarter of the time.

9 Cut the tongue-and-groove boards for the roof and screw them on to the timbers beneath. Allow a generous overlap to keep the interior dry.

10 Position the roofing felt across the top, and keep it in place with galvanized felt nails: these have large heads, which keep the felt firmly in place. I use an old batten with pencil markings to indicate the distance between them. It is surprising how much better a roof looks if the felt nails are evenly spaced and in line.

If you are good at wrapping parcels, then the corners will be no problem to you, but if not then practise on a scrap piece of felt. A Stanley knife is of great assistance in making tidy corner joints – yet another little detail that adds so much to a good-looking job.

DOORS

1 The twin doors are made next. Both are basically oblongs, each being made from four lengths of timber. The timbers are joined by long screws passing from the vertical pieces into the horizontal pieces. Carefully prepare the pilot holes in the vertical pieces, and use plenty of glue in the joints.

2 Now cut the shiplap boards to length and glue and nail them to the frame. Do not glue and nail them at their edges, but about 1½in (38mm) in: this will avoid splitting them. I decided not to add the traditional bracing bars, and the original pair of doors I made have not sagged.

3 Screw the T-strap hinges to the doors, and then attach the doors to the front corner posts. It is essential to use a hasp in the middle that has provision for a padlock.

FINISHING

Use a wood-care product as described on page 19. Here I have used Ronseal Quick-Drying Garden Woodstain in Terracotta. Be certain to lie the store on its back and treat the underneath generously with two coats before finally setting it upright.

Now comes the task of moving the store into its position in the garden. To do this, I cut two lengths of timber, gluing and screwing these on to the outside of the box. These timbers give points at which to lift. After the store has been sited, do not be surprised if the doors need some fine adjustments before they will open and close smoothly. When you move something this size, the framework will move slightly and adjustments will be necessary.

DECKING WITH HAND RAILS

Building a deck is well within the grasp of most DIYers. Although this is just a small deck, it uses all the techniques necessary for a much larger structure. It is a good idea to build a simple deck like this, learn from the experience, and then add on to it. The really significant item to watch out for with all decking is the ground work. If you have a flat area, then this is relatively simple, but if your garden slopes, beware: you can soon get into some seriously heavy preparatory digging.

Survey your patch, using a long batten of wood and a spirit level. This will tell you how much slope there is and how much 'making up' or digging out must be done. If the area has only a slight incline, you can fairly easily get the levels right using concrete blocks. If it is steeper, and you are still determined to have decking, hire a small excavator and its driver for a day. One of these mini diggers can dig, move and level more earth in a day than two men with picks and shovels can do in two weeks.

DIY stores can provide you with all you need for decking: boards, joists, balustrading clips, bolts, and so on. Most of the ready-made components you can buy are pressure-treated with a preservative. This is vital for a long-lasting deck. Once the decking is complete you can make it the colour you want.

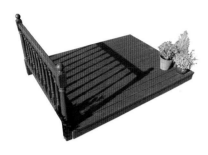

Dimensions

Height	36in (914mm)
Width	72in (1829mm)
Depth	98in (2489mm)

Tools

A big triangular builder's square – Stanley make a folding one. A spirit level about 18in (45cm) long – look for one with both horizontal and vertical vials. Pickaxe, shovel and wheelbarrow. The largest expanding rule you can afford (nothing less than 8ft/2.5m). Two hammers: a general-purpose 'lump' hammer and a claw hammer for driving in nails. Bosch drills – a battery drill/screwdriver is invaluable, along with a mains-powered drill for the large bolt holes – drill bits, countersink. Depending on the method of fixing for the deck boards, a Stanley Bostitch nail gun and a compressor are very useful. All these are available from a tool hire shop. Jetcut saw, ball of twine for aligning timbers, and a pair of rubber kneeling pads – to stop knobbly knees getting sore with all that kneeling.

Sundries

This will depend largely on the method that you choose to fix the decking boards, but screws, nails and bolts are all necessary – and all must be galvanized; you will also need glue, concrete blocks, and a wood-care product.

Timber

Most timber merchants now sell decking boards with machined surfaces for good grip, but if possible go to a specialist supplier who will provide you with everything you need. Besides the ground deck planks, you need newel posts at the ends, turned spindles and hand rails. You will find, with a little investigation, that suppliers of decking planks will not just keep all the parts needed, but the metal clips required to hold the hand rails to the newel posts.

Cutting List

Joists	6	60½ x 6 x 2in (1537 x 152 x 50mm)
Noggins	5	16½ x 6 x 2in (420 x 152 x 50mm)
Side boards	2	94¾ x 6 x 2in (2407 x 152 x 50mm)
Decking capping boards	2	94¾ x 5 x 1¼in (2407 x 127 x 32mm)
Decking boards	14	94¾ x 5 x 1¼in (2407 x 127 x 32mm)
Newel posts	2	size as sold
Spindles	9	size as sold
Hand rails	3	size as sold

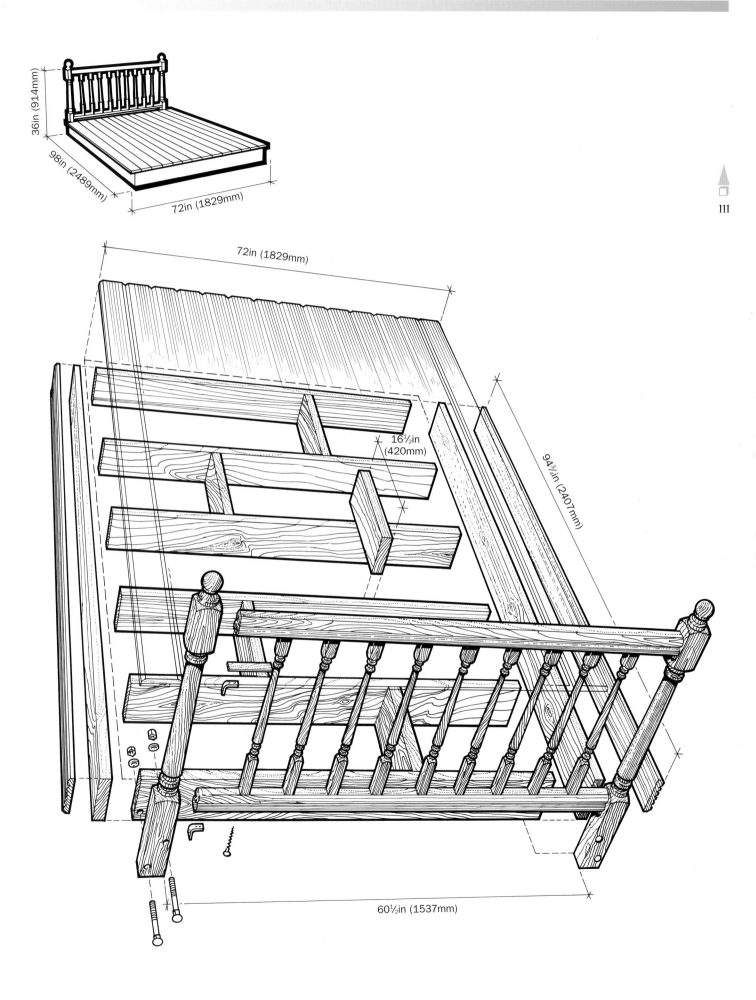

36in (914mm)

98in (2489mm)

72in (1829mm)

72in (1829mm)

16½in (420mm)

94¾in (2407mm)

60½in (1537mm)

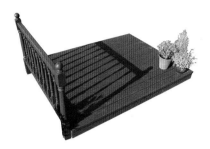

Construction

1 I like to keep my timbers off the ground. I know that pressure-treated timber will last 15–20 years, but I always think that it is kinder to keep it off the ground anyway, and allow the circulation of air beneath both the deck boards and their joists. To do this I buy some standard concrete blocks – the 4in (100mm) thick type are perfect for the job. Using the big square, I mark on the ground exactly where the deck will go, and where to place the blocks. Ideally there needs to be a block at the end of each joist and, depending on the span, one in the middle. For this small deck, one block at the end of each joist is more than adequate.

Cut the turf out where the blocks will need to go, if it hasn't already been removed during the ground-work phase, and inset each block into the ground by approximately 2in (100mm); again a square and spirit level are necessary. Remember to check that everything is level from one block to the next as you go. A long wooden batten, used in conjunction with the spirit level, is just perfect for this. Setting the concrete blocks in the ground and levelling them takes time and patience, but I really do feel that they are beneficial in the long run.

2 Now position the joists on the blocks. Ideally they should be positioned so their centres are 16in (406mm) apart. When I built my first deck, I screwed in roofing battens to hold the joists in place temporarily, before I fixed the decking planks. To prevent joists moving, short lengths of timber, called noggins, are introduced between them at right angles. You could probably get away without fixing noggins, but if you want to get things right, then put them in. To avoid shaking the structure, as nothing is strongly fixed together, it is a good idea to use a big Bosch drill/screwdriver to drive the screws through the joists into the noggins. Drill pilot holes in the joists first. For a quicker fix, use a nail gun, which will drive a nail straight through the joist and into the noggin at the touch of a button.

3 The next job is to fix the balustrade. The newel posts at each end are attached using nuts and bolts, so you need to do this before you put the decking planks in place.

Cramp a newel post to the end joist and drill the necessary bolt holes; these need to be off-centre, one at the top left-hand corner and the other at the bottom right-hand corner. It is a good idea to use a drill bit that is slightly larger than the bolt – it makes fitting the bolt much simpler. Bolt the newel posts to the joist, checking as you tighten up the nuts that it is upright. Don't forget the washers. Repeat for the other newel post.

4 Starting at one side, fix the decking planks. There are several ways to do this. These are your options:

a) Galvanized deck claws and galvanized nails. As each board is offered up, the claw holds the far side – in other words, you fix the boards without any nails or screws showing – very neat. The final board is anchored with screws.

b) Deck ties. These are made by Richard Burbidge and are particularly useful where complicated board patterns are envisaged. The method of fixing is fully illustrated in the Richard Burbidge catalogue, so I shall not describe it in detail.

c) **Secret screws.** Screws are driven in at 45 degrees to the side of the decking board. You will need to start the screw point a short way down the board so that when the screw is fully driven into place the head can not be seen. You will definitely need a Bosch battery screwdriver for this job.

d) **Stanley Bostitch air-tool nailer.** This is my favourite way of fixing decking boards. The nailer will drive nails straight into the decking planks and the joists below. It is a very quick and easy way to build your decking, and the most sensible if you are building a big deck. The whole system can be hired, along with a pair of safety specs. You must read all the safety instructions, and take care, but these guns save a lot of arm ache.

5 If you use method (**c**) or (**d**), make yourself a spacer batten (see page 24) to space the deck boards evenly. This avoids the tedium of measuring the gap each time. If for any reason your timbers are short, or you want to make full use of any off cuts, stagger the joints across the deck, otherwise you will introduce a weakness into the structure.

6 At the edges, it is necessary to cut a small section out of the deck boards to fit them around the newel posts. Do not forget to treat any cut ends with wood preservative, or water and the dreaded algae will get in and start the rotting process.

7 Now the spindles and hand rails need to be fitted. The Burbidge hand-rail system is all machined ready to take the spindles. Firstly, cut the hand rails to length (two for the top and one for the bottom). Take two of the rails (one top and one bottom) and place them side by side. Pencil in across both rails the positions for the screws that will hold the spindles to the rails. Bore screw pilot holes in these two hand rails.

8 Find a flat surface – a table or bench – and assemble all the spindles on it. Position the bottom rail along the bottom ends of the spindles. Make sure the 'dished' area is facing away from the spindles. The screws going into the spindles will have to grip into end grain, so they need to be fairly long – 2½in/63mm No. 8's are ideal.

9 The first top rail is next. This time the 'dished' area is fitted onto the spindles, and the screws are driven in from the top of the rail. Now comes the second of the top rails. This is used to hide all the screw holes. Fit it over the first top rail, with the 'dished' area downwards, and then drive screws from the underside to hold it in position.

10 The whole rail system can now be fixed to the newel posts with small screw clips (part of the Burbidge package).

11 Finally, fix the decking capping boards along each long edge of the deck to finish off neatly.

FINISHING

Although the decking is pre-treated with wood preservative, it is not a very attractive colour (tinges of green show through). Ronseal have specially formulated decking preservatives. The decking stain is hardwearing, semi-transparent and available in natural colours. It not only resists rain and damp conditions, but is also resistant to footwear scuffs and so on. Furthermore it also helps to prevent warping and twisting of deck boards, and the build-up of mildew.

ROOFED GARDEN TABLE

Sitting out in your garden is always a pleasure, but sitting out and having a meal – that is a bonus. I have designed many garden benches and tables, but this is the only one that has a roof – the roofed variety of table is perfect for when the weather is less than predictable. It not only keeps off the summer shower when you are eating, it also stops the hot sun melting the cheese and turning fresh bread sticks into rock cakes. To eat out successfully, you must have a table with a roof – nothing else will do!

I made my roofed table from Canadian white cedar, which came from Quebec and is grown and felled under some of the most strict conservation rules I have ever encountered. White cedar is virtually impervious to damp, so it is excellent for the project; however, Nordic spruce is a good alternative.

Cutting List

TABLE

Feet	4	71 x 4¾ x 2in (1803 x 121 x 50mm)
Roof legs	4	57½ x 5 x 2in (1460 x 127 x 50mm)
Bench legs	8	17x 4¾ x 2in (432 x 121 x 50mm)
Table legs	4	31 x 4¾ x 2in (787 x 121 x 50mm)
Central table rail	1	62 x 4¾ x 2in (1575 x 121 x 50mm)
Wedges	4	8 x 1½ x 1in (203 x 38 x 25mm)
Bench seat support (side)	4	48 x 2½ x 1¾in (1219 x 63 x 44mm)
Bench seat support (end)	4	17 x 2½ x 1¾in (432 x 63 x 44mm)
Bench seat support (cross rail)	4	7 x 2½ x 1¾in (178 x 63 x 44mm)
Table support (side)	2	47¾ x 2¾ x 1¾in (1213 x 63 x 44mm)
Table support (cross rail)	2	20¼ x 2¾ x 1¾in (514 x 63 x 44mm)
Table ends	2	24 x 4¾ x 2in (610 x 121 x 50mm)
Bench slats	6	60 x 3¾ x ¾in (1524 x 95 x 19mm)
Table top slats	7	60 x 3¾ x ¾in (1524 x 95 x 19mm)

BENCH BACKS

Bench backs	24	34 x 2¾ x ¾in (864 x 70 x 19mm)
Bench back supports	6	44 x 3 x 1½in (1118 x 76 x 38mm)

ROOF

Roof (WBP plywood)	2	61¼ x 51 x ¾in (1683 x 1295 x 19mm)
Roof frame (verticals)	4	47½ x 2¾ x 1¾in (1206 x 70 x 44mm)
Roof frame (horizontals)	4	48 x 2¾ x 1¾in (1219 x 70 x 44mm)
Roof frame (inner horizontals)	2	48 x 2¾ x ⅞in (1219 x 70 x 22mm)
Shingles		these are sold as bales – see tip
Barge boards	4	51 x 2 x ⅞in (1295 x 50 x 22mm)

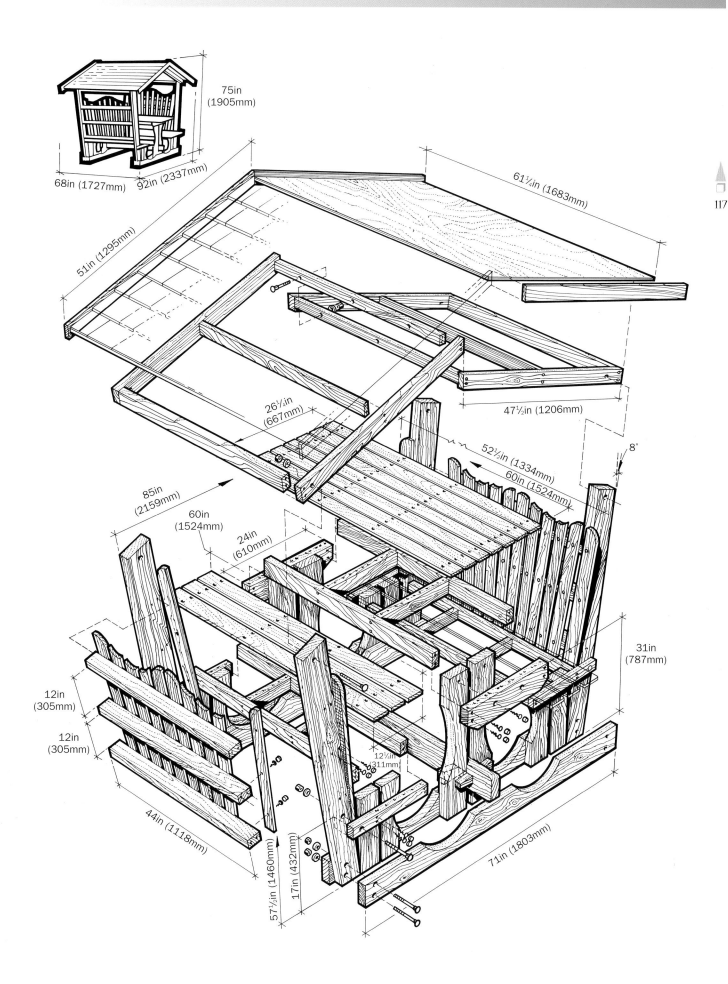

75in
(1905mm)

68in (1727mm)

92in (2337mm)

61¼in (1683mm)

51in (1295mm)

47½in (1206mm)

26¼in
(667mm)

52½in (1334mm)

60in
(1524mm)

8°

85in
(2159mm)

60in
(1524mm)

24in
(610mm)

31in
(787mm)

12in
(305mm)

12in
(305mm)

12¼in
(311mm)

44in (1118mm)

57½in (1460mm)

17in (432mm)

71in (1803mm)

Dimensions

Height   75in (1905mm)
Width   92in (2337mm)
Depth   68in (1727mm)

Tools

Pencil, expanding rule, carpenter's square. All your hand tools: Bosch battery drill/screwdriver, large drill bits, countersink, Bosch jigsaw, Jetcut saw. You will find the Stanley Bostitch air tools perfect for fixing the shingle tiles.

Sundries

Several boxes of zinc-plated screws (1^1/$_2$in/38mm, No. 8), coach bolts, copper nails (for the shingles), glue, wood-care product.

Timber

The table is Canadian white cedar, as are the tiles. They are cut on the taper, and form a very substantial roof. When freshly sawn, they are a really delightful dull red-brown, but this fades after 18 months, so it is best to use a wood stain, even though they will not rot.

If white cedar is not available, the best alternative is Nordic spruce. You may have difficulty getting the larger-sized timbers, but most timber merchants will be happy to help. Do not forget to go armed with the cutting list.

Tips

At certain stages, namely fixing the roof, you will need an assistant or two to hold the timbers while you drill and fix. This is a very heavy table and you will need a minimum of two men to do so – and if you have to lift it up steps or move it any distance, one person on each corner is a must.

The shingles are sold in bales, and different manufacturers sell different size shingles in different size bales, so it is really a matter of try and see.

Study the diagram carefully and familiarize yourself with all the table parts before you start. You will need a long weekend to get the job completed; you'll also need plenty of space, so either clean up the workshop or use the double garage.

Construction
TABLE

1 Start with the feet and legs as these form the main structure of the table. The feet consist of four horizontal lengths of timber, two each side. Between each pair are 'trapped' eight uprights: two that hold the roof, four that form the legs for the benches and two table legs – look at the diagram to see how this works.

Mark out and cut the four lengths of timber for the feet. Do the same for the corresponding

16 lengths that form all the legs. With all these varying lengths of timber around it is not a bad idea to pencil in which is which, or put them in piles – mistakes are annoying, and costly.

2 Lay one foot out on a flat surface. Now take one set of legs: two roof legs, four bench legs and two table legs. Position these on the foot. It helps to make a central pencil line – the point between the table legs – and work outwards from here. Don't forget to allow space between the table legs for the central rail (see step 5). The roof legs are offset at 8 degrees, so mark this in clearly on the timber – you will need to remove a small angle at the base of the roof legs before fitting them to the structure. Once you are happy that all the legs are in the right place, pencil in their positions. Transfer the markings onto one of the feet that will make up the other side to ensure a matching pair.

3 As you now know the position of the bench and table legs, you can pencil in the semi-circular cut-aways that allow foot access to the table. Using a jigsaw with a Bosch Progressor blade, cut these out on all four feet. Don't forget to clamp the pieces firmly in place before you start cutting. The

Progressor blade gives an excellent finish, so you will not need to use glasspaper or a spokeshave to remove the saw marks.

4 Now reassemble a set of two feet and eight legs, with the legs sandwiched between the pair of feet. This is a bit of a handful, so have some clamps ready to hold the timbers while you position them. It's well worth having a rehearsal to make sure that everything will work out. If it looks like a roof rack for a camel, check the diagram before going any further! When you are ready to glue and screw the ends together, get help from an assistant. Use glue and screws or coach bolts (see diagram) and, at every opportunity, check against the pencilled lines you have made. Screws should be driven in from both sides to hold the leg sandwich together. Now repeat the process for the other group of feet and legs.

5 With both ends made up, they now have to be joined together. One of the major timbers to do this job is the central table rail, which fits between the table legs and has mortice holes to take wedges. However, the first job is to get the central rail to fit between the legs – you may have to plane the ends to reduce the thickness of the timber slightly.

6 Once you have the rail fitting snugly between the table legs, and evenly at both ends, mark in pencil the position for the mortice holes on either side of the legs and at both ends. I decided to have twin wedges at each end as these exert tremendous clamping power on the table legs, when driven in. They also give rigidity to the lower part of the structure.

Remove the rail from between the legs and make full pencil marks for the positions of all four mortice holes on both sides of it. Cut the holes with a firmer chisel and mallet, and work on a firm bench. The holes need to be on a slight angle, to correspond with the angle of the wooden wedges that will go through them (see step 7). Cut each hole from both sides. Don't be tempted to cut only from one side, there will be a tendency for the chisel to break through, creating some nasty splinters.

7 Cut your four wedges; use a smoothing plane to shape them up. Test out the wedges in the holes before assembling them in the table (step 9).

8 From the diagram, you will see that there are support battens that go under the table and both benches – six for each

bench and four for the table. Cut these to length. Also cut the table ends, not forgetting to shape these.

9 With your two assistants, get one to hold each end, leaving your hands free to insert the central table rail between the table legs. Drive the wedges in temporarily, then check that both table ends are upright, ie at 90 degrees to the ground. Your assistants can then fully drive in the wedges. Do not over drive them, just do enough to hold the legs firmly.

10 Next assemble the bench seat supports before asking your assistants to hold them in place over the bench legs while you glue and screw them in place. Use coach bolts to fasten them to the roof legs (see diagram). Do the same for the other side, and then check once again that the table ends are still at 90 degrees to the ground. Stanley spirit levels have vials for both flat and upright, so it is quite simple to keep a check of progress.

11 Screw the shaped table ends in place, and then add the table supports between them. The more supports you fix between both ends of the table, the stronger and more rigid the structure becomes.

12 Cut the bench seat slats. Round off the ends to prevent accidents, before both gluing and screwing the slats in place. Fix the cross rails on the table top, and then cut and fix the table top slats in place. Again, smoothing off the end edges avoids accidents. I don't like to see screw heads, so I use a matching countersink drill and a wooden plug cutter for the table top and bench seats. The screws are inserted, the holes have a dab of glue put in, and then the wood plugs are driven into them. Use a sharp chisel to cut off the protruding plug. Stanley make a whole range of plug cutters for this sort of application. A word of warning: don't be tempted to use dowel rod for the purpose, it will always show because the dowel rod is end grain.

BENCH BACKS

1 The bench backs are supported by three timbers on each side. Cut these out, and glue and screw them into place on the roof legs.

2 Now make the bench back slats. I cut a paper pattern of the shape at the top and mark this on to the timbers before cutting them with a jigsaw. Make sure all the ends are rounded off, including the bench and table

ends. This avoids anyone hurting themselves. Perhaps the simplest method of fixing the back slats is to screw the middle one in first, then the two outer ones, before positioning the ones in between. If you find it difficult to keep the flow of the curve under control, use some Blu-Tack on the backs of the slats to hold them in place until you are satisfied, then make pencil marks on them, showing exactly how they should go. Glue and screw them in place.

ROOF

1 The roof is formed from a framework of batten and WBP plywood. Cut the framework battens to length. Glue and screw them together. Make the holes for the coach bolts that will hold the two frames together at the apex. Now glue and screw the plywood to the frames.

2 With the help of your valuable assistants, lift the roof in place. Fix the coach bolts in the apex of the roof to hold the roof sections together. When these are in place, bolt the corners of the roof to the four roof legs. This is quickly and easily written, but in practice it is inevitable that some cutting and a little planing will be necessary before everything fits well – be prepared to take the roof on and off a few times.

3 Now the roof shingles are fixed, using copper nails and starting at the bottom and working up to the apex. Initially install a double thickness, setting the second row back only $1/2$in (13mm) or so. This builds up the edge, ensuring better rain shedding. The rest of the roof is single thickness. You must stagger the joints, so that water running off one tile runs onto a 'full' one beneath. Each row of tiles covers up the copper nails from the last row.

4 Once the roof is fixed, barge boards are fitted to the outside edges.

FINISHING

Use a wood-care product as described on page 19. I used Ronseal Garden Woodstain – I like the colour Bilberry, but the choice is yours.

TOOL STORE

Perhaps it is a luxury to have a place for everything and everything in its place, but it makes life simpler and less frustrating. Several projects in this book support such an ideal, this one included. It will house long-handled garden tools and keep tidy other equipment. And at least it is somewhere to keep the rake hung up and so prevent the classic nose-smacking event as your wellied foot accidentally activates the handle to 'sock you one'.

Cutting List

FLOOR

Bearers (side)	2	25¼ x 2 x 2in (641 x 50 x 50mm)
Bearers (front and back)	2	30 x 2 x 2in (762 x 50 x 50mm)
Floorboards (T&G)	6	34 x 4½ x ¾in (864 x 114 x 19mm)

SHED FRAME

Frame verticals, including door	6	62½ x 2 x 2in (1587 x 50 x 50mm)
Door spacers (noggins)	2	4⅜ x 2 x 2in (111 x 50 x 50mm)
Door jamb	1	62½ x 2 x ⅞in (1587 x 50 x 22mm)
Frame side horizontals	4	21½ x 2 x 2in (546 x 50 x 50mm)
Frame front and back horizontals	4	35 x 2 x 2in (889 x 50 x 50mm)
Frame back centre horizontal	1	30½ x 2 x 2in (774 x 50 x 50mm)

ROOF FRAME

Eaves	2	36¼ x 2 x 2in (921 x 50 x 50mm)
Main timbers	2	34 x 2 x 2in (864 x 50 x 50mm)
Main timbers	2	32 x 2 x 2in (813 x 50 x 50mm)
Apex	1	19¾ x 2 x 2in (502 x 50 x 50mm)
Internal triangle	2	4 x 4 x 2in (102 x 102 x 50mm)
Fitting blocks	4	4 x 2 x 2in (102 x 50 x 50mm)
Barge boards	4	35 x 2 x 2in (889 x 50 x 50mm)
External triangle	2	4 x 4 x ⅞in (102 x 102 x 22mm)
Finials	2	14 x 3 x ⅞in (356 x 76 x 22mm)

SHIPLAP

Back	16	35¼ x 4½ x ⅝in (895 x 114 x 16mm)
Back apex	4 cut to fit frame from 4½ x ⅝in (114 x 16mm)	
Front	30	9½ x 4½ x ⅝in (241 x 114 x 16mm)
Front lintel	1	35 x 4½ x ⅝in (889 x 114 x 16mm)
Front apex	5 cut to fit frame from 4½ x ⅝in (114 x 16mm)	
Sides	32	26½ x 4½ x ⅝in (673 x 114 x 16mm)
Roof	16	36¼ x 4½ x ⅝in (921 x 114 x 16mm)

DOOR

Door (T&G)	4	62 x 4¼ x ⅝in (1575 x 108 x 16mm)
Horizontal braces	3	17 x 3 x ⅞in (432 x 76 x 22mm)
Diagonal braces	2	28 x 3 x ⅞in (711 x 76 x 22mm)

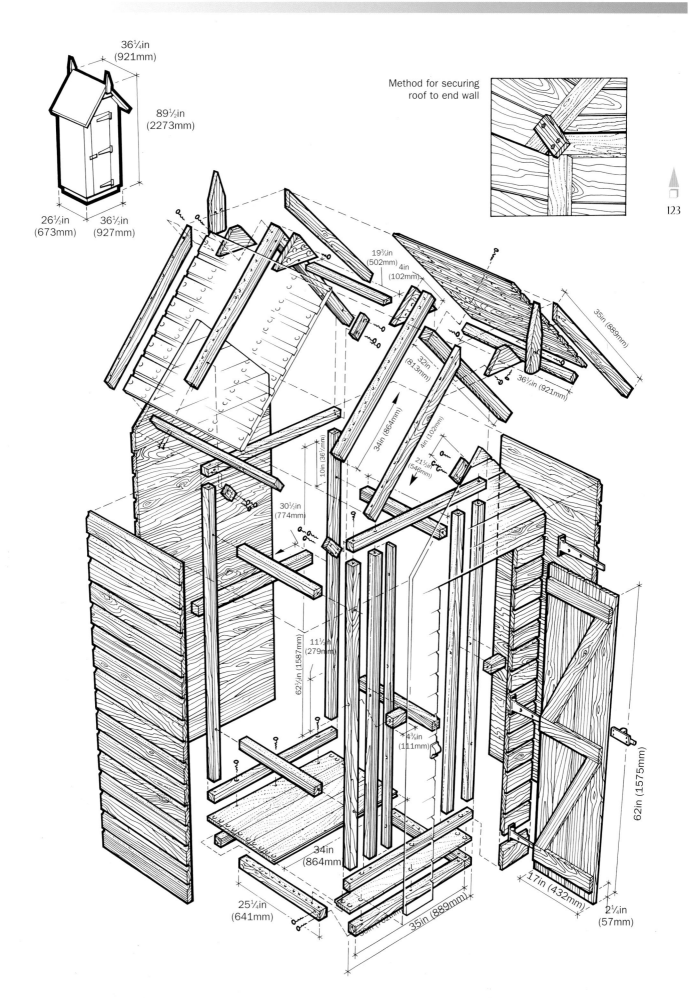

36¼in
(921mm)

89½in
(2273mm)

26½in
(673mm)

36½in
(927mm)

Method for securing
roof to end wall

19¾in
(502mm)

4in
(102mm)

35in (889mm)

32in
(813mm)

36¼in (921mm)

34in (864mm)

4in (102mm)

21½in
(546mm)

10in (367mm)

30½in
(774mm)

11¼in
(279mm)

62½in (1587mm)

4⅜in
(111mm)

62in (1575mm)

34in
(864mm)

25¼in
(641mm)

35in (889mm)

17in (432mm)

2¼in
(57mm)

Dimensions

Height	89$\frac{1}{2}$in (2273mm)
Width	36$\frac{1}{2}$in (927mm)
Depth	26$\frac{1}{2}$in (673mm)

Tools

Pencil, expanding rule, carpenter's square, protractor or sliding bevel gauge, Jetcut saw, Bosch battery drill/screwdriver, drill bits, countersink, antivibe hammer, Bosch circular saw. A Stanley Bostitch nailer makes quick work of fixing the shiplap boards.

Sundries

Screws (1$\frac{1}{2}$in/38mm, No. 8 and 2in/50mm, No. 8), oval nails, 'T'-strap hinges 9in (229mm), bolt or hasp, nails, glue, wood-care product.

Timber

All the framework is 2 x 2in (50 x 50mm) timber, and you can save money by choosing the sawn variety, or use a Bosch planer and plane it up yourself – which will make a big saving. The cladding is shiplap board. And there is a small quantity of tongue-and-groove floor boarding.

Construction

FLOOR

1 Cut the floor bearers to length, and glue and screw them together. I always make the base first, and from this take the exact dimensions for the front, and back and sides. When you measure for these, allow for a little slack; do not make the floor too tight a fit on the base.

2 Now cut the tongue-and-groove floor boarding to length. Remove the tongue from one end board and the groove from the other, for neatness. Screw the boards to the floor frame.

STORE

1 Cut the timbers for the front and back frame and glue and screw them together, following the diagram. The front frame requires more work than the rear as you have to form a door frame, but this is fairly straightforward. To prevent the door frame flexing, a couple of short lengths of timber, or noggins, are glued between the door frame and the outer frame.

2 With the back and front framework built now cut the shiplap boards to length. This is a repetitive job so it is worth making a short batten as a measuring stick. You must cut the ends of the boards square. To minimise waste, save any short ends for fitting around the door frame.

3 Before you start fitting the shiplap, check for the squareness of each frame. Use oval nails as they are less likely to split the ends. Nailing all the shiplap is a lot of work, so you might like to consider buying one of Stanley's 'antivibe' hammers (see page 7). They take the vibration away from your joints and will help prevent tennis elbow. Alternatively, the Stanley compressor-driven nailing gun makes light work of this. You can hire one from your local tool hire shop.

4 Once you have completed the back and front, start on the sides (shaping the apex pieces comes later). Fix horizontal battens between the front and back frames: two each side will make a more stable framework. The structure is quite large and you should get someone to help you turn it over. Check that the shed stays square as you hammer on the shiplap sides.

ROOF

1 To make the roof, cut the four main roof timbers, join them together and screw two fairly substantial timber triangles to them. This gives the shiplap timbers a framework to keep them together.

2 Fit the roof timbers to the shed frame, using the inset picture on the diagram as a guide. You will need to screw the fitting blocks (see inset diagram) in place before further work can continue. Get a helper to hold the triangular roofing timber while you check alignment and drive in the screws.

3 Cut the shiplap roof timbers to length and screw these to the roof frame. It is important to screw these boards, as hammering would shake the structure. To avoid the screws going straight through the shiplap and missing the timbers beneath, draw in pencil lines on the top side to show you exactly where to drive them. Once the screws are all in place you will be amazed at how rigid the roof has become.

APEX – FRONT AND BACK

1 Now fix the apex shiplap boards to the outside faces of the roof timbers. First cut them to fit. Be careful to mark each piece with the correct angles. Take time over these – the end result will be worth it. It i s best to screw these in place, rather than nail them.

2 Cut and screw the barge boards on to the front and back faces of the roof. From waste wood shape the finials; I don't know their purpose, but no shed looks right without them. Screw them in place.

DOOR

1 Cut to length the door timbers and the three horizontal braces. It is the horizontal braces that hold a simple door like this together. The diagonal braces need to be cut a little over length to allow for the angles that have to be cut on their ends.

2 For neatness, remove the tongue from one outside board and the groove from the other outside board, before assembling the tongue-and-groove timbers, making sure they are slotted together tightly. On the outside of the door, pencil in where the braces will go on the inside. Lie the door down and position the braces under it, checking the alignment of the pencil lines (this is a bit of a fiddle). Screw through the door into the braces beneath.

3 Turn the door over to fit the two diagonal braces, which will stop the door from sagging. It is important that these braces start at the side of the door where the hinges are. Using the horizontal timbers as a guide, pencil in the exact angles to be cut on the diagonal braces. Cut the angles and then screw the diagonals in place from the outside.

4 Now fit the 'T'-strap hinges. It is probably easiest to fit them to the door and then to the store. Next, fit the door into the frame. First glue and screw the thin liner to the door jam. To stop the door sticking in its opening, wedge two pieces of thick card or thin timber offcuts at its base as you screw in the hinges. Remove these once the hinges are in place and the door will swing easily. Don't make the door too tight in the frame as when the wood gets damp, it will stick.

5 Fit a good strong hasp. It is a good idea to have one that makes provision for a padlock. For added security, choose one that is designed in such a way as to cover the attaching screw heads when the padlock is locked. This will foil the enterprising burglar who comes equipped with a screwdriver.

FINISHING

Before you set up the tool store in the garden, pay particular attention to the underneath of the floor. Give this at least three coats of woodstain (see page 19). Here I have used Ronseal Quick-Drying Garden Woodstain in Terracotta for the roof, Evergreen for the walls and Harvest Gold for the door.

SUPPLIERS

Listed below are the UK companies who supplied me with tools or products for this book, many of which have very helpful enquiry lines and websites. Readers in the US will find the additional addresses useful when sourcing tools and materials.

UK

Hozelock Cyprio Ltd
Haddenham
Aylesbury
Buckinghamshire
HP17 8JD
tel: 01844 291881
website: www.hozelock.com

Robert Bosch Ltd
Power Tools Division
PO Box 98
Uxbridge
Middlesex
UB9 5HJ
tel: 01895 838743
website: www.bosch.co.uk

Richard Burbidge Ltd
Whittington Road
Oswestry
Shropshire
SY11 1HZ
tel: 01691 655131
fax: 01691 657694
email:info@richardburbidge.co.uk
website:www.richardburbidge.co.uk

Screwfix Direct
FREEPOST
Yeovil
Somerset
BA22 8BF
tel: 0500 414141
fax: 0800 056 2256
email: online@screwfix.com
website: www.screwfix.com

Stanley Tools
Drakehouse Office
Brighton Road East
Drakehouse
Sheffield
S20 7JZ
tel: 08701 650650
fax: 08701 654764
website: www.stanleyworks.com

UHU Group
Grove House
551 London Road
Isleworth
Middlesex
TW7 4DS
tel: 020 8847 2227
fax: 020 8569 8530
email: uhuuk@aol.com
website: www.uhu-uk.co.uk

United Sawmills (UK) Ltd
Stags End House
Gaddesdon
Row
Hemel Hempstead
Herts
HP2 6HX1
tel: 01582 791400

Paskett Public Relations Ltd
50/51 Frier Gate
Derby
DE1 1DF
(agents for Qualcast who supplied the mower and shredder)
email: info@paskett
website: www.paskett.co.uk

Ronseal Ltd
Thorncliffe Park
Chapeltown
Sheffield
S35 2YP
tel: 0114 246 7171
fax: 0114 245 5629
email: enquiry@ronseal.co.uk
website: www.ronseal.co.uk

US

Garret Wade Co
161 Avenue of the America
New York 10013
tel: 800 221 2942
email: mail@garrettwade.com
website: www.garrettwade.com

Lee Valley Tools Ltd
Ogdensburg
New York
tel: 800 871 8158
website: www.leevalley.com

Rockler Woodworking and Hardware
4365 willow Drive
Medina
Minnesota 55340
tel: 800 279 4441
email: support@rockler.com
website: www.rockler.com

Sikkens Decorative Wood Finishes
Troy
Michigan
800 833 7288
tel: 8000 833 7288
email: sikkensnam@akzonobel.com
website: www.sikkens.com

Wolfcraft Inc
1222 West Ardmore Avenue
PO Box 687
Itasca
Illinois
tel: 630 773 4777
fax: 630 773 4805
email: agnes.norberciak@woawolfcraft.com
website:www.wolfcraft.com

ACKNOWLEDGMENTS

One of the most positive things about writing and creating the projects for a new book is the people you meet, who so willingly give of their time and expertise to help you. No author is the fount of all knowledge, and so as this book has progressed, I have learnt a great deal from you all. Thank you for your help, encouragement, enthusiasm and patience.
Patricia, my wife, who processed all my text.
Mark Jarvis and Steve Jenkins at Perception Photography, who showed great patience in juggling the pictures between the days of rain and overcast skies.
Keith Field, the illustrator, whose quite brilliant three-dimensional drawings make the practical side of construction so much simpler.
John Roberts and Claire Brewer at Bosch Power Tools, whose advice, expertise and encouragement I found invaluable, and Alan R MacDonald, Marketing Director.
Jonathan Lloyd of Curtis Brown, who should really be in the diplomatic service!
Stephen Gibson, James Smith and Angela Mulcahy of Ronseal – great finishes, but next time bring some brushes!
John Philips and Emma Morrish of UHU.
Martyn Whybrow, Ray Smith and Gary Carter at Richard Burbidge, who did some wonderful carving for me!
Stanley Tools – Elizabeth Blades and Graham Bennett – thank you both, and Alan Hampshire, who has taught me all I know about air tools, as well as Clive Mears, who keeps an eye on us.
Graham Paskett and Rachel Evans of Paskett Public Relations Ltd, who made possible the loan of a Qualcast Rotary Mower and the Atco Quiet Shredder for two of the projects.
Trevor Culpin of Screwfix direct, who not surprisingly knows all there is to know about screws and many other tools besides.
Hozelock Cyprio, who supplied the pump for the Pebble Pool and the Old Village Pump. Special thanks to Simon Chapman for a superb service and lots of advice.
Fiona Eaton, Sara Domville and Miranda Spicer at David and Charles.
Jo Weeks, the editor, who painstakingly checked text, drawings and cutting lists, to see that it all worked.
The management of Jardinerie Garden Centres, Stonehouse. Thank you for the loan of the plants and to Louise Powell who helped with styling.

127

INDEX